Peculiar Treasures

Other Books by Frederick Buechner

FICTION

A Long Day's Dying
The Seasons' Difference
The Return of Ansel Gibbs
The Final Beast
The Entrance to Porlock
Lion Country
Open Heart
Love Feast
Treasure Hunt
The Book of Bebb
Godric
Brendan
The Wizard's Tide
The Son of Laughter

NONFICTION

The Magnificent Defeat
The Hungering Dark
The Alphabet of Grace
Wishful Thinking: A Seeker's ABC
The Faces of Jesus
Telling the Truth: The Gospel as
Tragedy, Comedy, and Fairy Tale
The Sacred Journey
Now and Then
A Room Called Remember
Whistling in the Dark: A Doubter's Dictionary
Telling Secrets
The Clown in the Belfry

Peculiar Treasures

A Biblical *Who's Who*

Frederick Buechner

With Illustrations by Katherine A. Buechner

HarperOne
An Imprint of HarperCollinsPublishers

HarperOne

PECULIAR TREASURES: *A Biblical Who's Who.* Text copyright © 1979 by Frederick Buechner. Illustrations copyright © 1979 by Katherine A. Buechner. All rights reserved. Printed in the United States of America. No part of this book may be used or reproduced in any manner whatsoever without written permission except in the case of brief quotations embodied in critical articles and reviews. For information, address HarperCollins Publishers, 195 Broadway, New York, NY 10007.

HarperCollins books may be purchased for educational, business, or sales promaotional use. For information, please e-mail the Special Markets Department at SPsales@harpercollins.com.

HarperCollins Web site: http://www.harpercollins.com
HarperCollins®, 📖®, and HarperOne™ are trademarks of HarperCollins Publishers.

Library of Congress Cataloging-in-Publication Data

Buechner, Frederick.
    Peculiar Treasures
    1. Bible—Biography. I. Title.
ISBN 978–0–06–061141–5
BS571.B84   220.9'2
[B]   92–54775

HB 09.11.2018

*Ye shall be a peculiar treasure unto me above all people,
for all the earth is mine.*

EXODUS 19:5

Contents

Author's Note

A few years ago I wrote a book called *Wishful Thinking: A Theological ABC*, in which I tried to shake a little of the dust off a lot of moth-eaten old religious words and put some color back in their cheeks. It was my plan in this book to try the same stunt with a lot of the moth-eaten old saints, prophets, potentates, and assorted sinners who roam through the pages of the Bible, but what I got for my presumption was exactly the reverse. Who did I think was moth-eaten? They were the ones who shook the dust off me, as things turned out, and if there's any color either in my cheeks or in these pages, it's mostly because they put it there.

Again and again I would start out thinking I knew who they were and what I wanted them to say for me, and again and again they dug in their heels. Not only did they refuse to be who I thought they were and insist on being themselves instead, but more often than not what I ended up saying about them were the words that they put in my mouth. Take Sarah, for instance. "After I have grown old and my husband is old, shall I have pleasure?" she says when the angel tells her she's going to have a baby at last, and I thought this was my chance to defend the view that the Lord blesses sex not just as the best way to keep up the birth rate but as a lot of fun too. Sarah would have none of it. Laughter, not sex, was what she insisted on my talking about, and for the views expressed under her name she must bear the major responsibility.

There's a fair amount of laughter elsewhere among these sketches too, and I'm prepared to have a lot of people say that it's unseemly at best and, at worst, enough to get me defrocked. All I can offer by way of defense is that the Bible itself has a great deal more laughter in it than all those double columns and black leatherette bindings would lead you to believe. I challenge anybody to deny that there was at least a smile on the lips of the ancient narrator who wrote that after the Queen of Sheba's staggering tour of King Solomon's palace, "There was no more spirit in her," and I doubt that Jesus himself kept an entirely straight face when he said it was easier for a camel to pass through the eye of a needle than for a rich man to enter Paradise. Easier for Nelson Rockefeller to pass through the night deposit slot of the Chase Manhattan Bank would seem to me a reasonable modern equivalent. But far richer than that is the kind of high and holy laughter Sarah steered me to, and that can be read about in the proper place.

Although I'm sure there's enough to start at least one fight on every page, I've tried to be as faithful to the spirit if not always the letter of Scripture as I could, using the Revised Standard Version in most cases with occasional forays into the King James. Where I've paraphrased passages or translated them into contemporary Americanese, I think I've at least stuck to the basic facts. Where I've transposed scenes from ancient Israel to more familiar settings, I hope my anachronisms are preposterous enough not to leave anybody with the impression that either my intent was to deceive or I just didn't know any better. Much as I dislike reading a text littered with bracketed scriptural references—it's like listening to somebody with a bad stutter—I have almost everywhere put them in to identify direct quotations. And except in the case of people like Moses, Jesus, and Paul, whose stories are scattered through many books, I have indicated at the end of each sketch the particular passages it was based on.

What struck me more than anything else as I reacquainted myself with this remarkable rag-bag of people was both their extraordinary aliveness and their power to make me feel somehow more alive myself for having known them. Even across all the centuries, they still have the power to bring tears to the eyes and send shivers up the spine. And more besides. Saints and scoundrels, nabobs and nobodies, they galvanize all the pages they appear on, and if this book serves to send people back to those pages themselves, so much the better. Beyond that, all I can say is that if it is only one tenth as much fun to read as it was to write, then I will be well pleased. My hope is that the reader will be too.

Aa

AARON

Moses was three years younger than his brother Aaron, but starting with the day Pharaoh's daughter fished him out of the bulrushes and adopted him, Moses was the one who always got the headlines while Aaron got the short end of the stick. Even when Moses had to clear out of Egypt for doing in an Egyptian Jew-baiter, he landed on his feet by marrying the daughter of a well-heeled sheep rancher across the border.

Aaron, in the meanwhile, went quietly off into the ministry where in the long run he didn't do so badly either except that the only people who knew about it were the ones who turned to the religion section on the back pages. Moses, on the other hand, was forever making the cover. The pay-off came around the time Moses hit eighty and out of a burning bush God himself voted him Man of the Year. As usual, Aaron had to be content with playing second fiddle, which

1

he did well enough until he got the break he'd been waiting for at last, and he blew it.

With Moses lingering so long on Mount Sinai that some thought he'd settled down and gone into real estate, the people turned to Aaron for leadership, and in no time flat—despite an expensive theological education and all those years in denominational headquarters—he had them dancing around the Golden Calf like a bunch of aborigines.

Nobody knows whether this was Aaron's way of getting even with his kid brother for all those years of eating humble pie, or whether he actually believed with the rest of mankind that a God in the hand is worth two in the bush.

(Exodus 32:1–4)

ABEL (*See* CAIN)

ABISHAG

When King David was nearing the end of his days, not even his electric blanket could fend off the ominous chill he felt rising in his bones. The fires of life were all but out, and in an effort to rekindle them for the old man and at the same

time preserve their own jobs, the establishment enlisted the aid of a beautiful young woman named Abishag. In the hope that she if anybody could start his blood coursing again, they persuaded her to join him in the sack. By this time, however, the old man was past rising to the occasion, and not long afterwards—perhaps as the result of his unsuccessful attempts to do so—he died. When one of his sons offered to make an honest woman of Abishag by marrying her, the establishment turned him down on the grounds that by taking over his father's girl friend, he was just making a play for taking over his father's throne. What finally became of Abishag is not recorded, and perhaps it is just as well.

This sad story makes it clear that in peace as well as in war there's no tragic folly you can't talk a nation's youth into simply by calling it patriotic duty.

(1 Kings 1–2)

ABRAHAM (See also HAGAR, ISAAC, SARAH)

If a *schlemiel* is a person who goes through life spilling soup on people and a *schlemozzle* is the one it keeps getting spilled on, then Abraham was a *schlemozzle*. It all began when God told him to go to the land of Canaan where he promised to make him the father of a great nation and he went.

The first thing that happened was that his brother-in-law Lot (q.v.) took over the rich bottom-land and Abraham was left with the scrub country around Dead Man's Gulch. The second thing was that the prospective father of a great nation found out his wife couldn't have babies. The third thing was that when, as a special present on his hundredth birthday, God arranged for his wife Sarah to have a son anyway, it wasn't long before he told Abraham to go up into the hills and sacrifice him (see ISAAC). It's true that at the last minute God stepped in and said he'd only wanted to see if the old man's money was where his mouth was, but from that day

forward Abraham had a habit of breaking into tears at odd moments, and his relationship with his son Isaac was never close.

In spite of everything, however, he never stopped having faith that God was going to keep his promise about making him the father of a great nation. Night after night, it was the dream he rode to sleep on—the glittering cities, the up-to-date armies, the curly-bearded kings. There was a group photograph he had taken not long before he died. It was a bar mitzvah, and they were all there down to the last poor relation. They weren't a great nation yet by a long shot, but you'd never know it from the way Abraham sits enthroned there in his velvet yarmulke with several great-grandchildren on his lap and soup on his tie.

Even through his thick lenses, you can read the look of faith in his eye, and more than all the kosher meals, the Ethical Culture Societies, the shaved heads of the women, the achievements of Maimonides, Einstein, Kissinger, it was that look that God loved him for and had chosen him for in the first place.

"They will all be winners, God willing. Even the losers will be winners. They'll all get their names up in lights," say the old schlemozzle's eyes.

"Someday—who knows when?—I'll be talking about my son, the Light of the world."

(Genesis 12–18, 22)

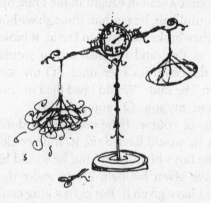

ABSALOM

Almost from the start, Absalom had a number of strikes against him. For one thing, he was much too handsome for his own good, and his special pride was such a magnificent head of hair that once a year when he had it trimmed, the trimmings alone tipped the scales at three and a half pounds. For another thing, his father, King David, was always either spoiling him rotten or reading him the riot act. This did not promote stability of character. He murdered his lecherous brother Amnon for fooling around with their sister Tamar, and when the old war-horse Joab wouldn't help him patch things up with David afterwards, he set fire to his hay field. All Israel found this kind of derring-do irresistible, of course, and when he eventually led a revolt against his father, a lot of them joined him.

On the eve of the crucial battle, David was a wreck. If he was afraid he might lose his throne, he was even more afraid he might lose Absalom. The boy was the thorn in his flesh, but he was also the apple of his eye, and before the fighting started, he told the chiefs of staff till they were sick of hearing it that if Absalom fell into their clutches, they must promise to go easy on him for his father's sake. Remembering what had happened to his hay field, old Joab kept his fingers crossed, and when he found Absalom caught in the branches of an oak tree by his beautiful hair, he ran him through without blinking an eye. When they broke the news to David, it broke his heart, just as simple as that, and he cried out in words that have echoed down the centuries ever since. "O my son Absalom, my son, my son," he said. "Would I had died instead of you, O Absalom, my son, my son" (2 Samuel 18:33).

He meant it, of course. If he could have done the boy's dying for him, he would have done it. If he could have paid the price for the boy's betrayal of him, he would have paid it. If he could have given his own life to make the boy alive again, he would have given it. But even a king can't do things like that. As later history was to prove, it takes a God.

(2 Samuel 13–19)

ADAM (*See also* EVE)

He let the *Times* fall to the carpet beside him. It was the usual recital—a new tax plan, the danger of oral contraceptives to women over forty, the mayor's special committee on child abuse. He pushed his glasses back on his forehead and with his thumb and forefinger massaged the loose flesh under his eyes. Through the club window he could see a fat woman in slacks waiting for a bus, a boy with a pony tail walking a dog. Somebody had the TV on in another room, and he could hear the rise and fall of canned laughter. He lit a cigarette and let the smoke drift out of his mouth without exhaling it. The city sky was turning brown with the approach of dusk. Then suddenly, as if it had been only yesterday, he remembered Eden.

The leopard . . . the starling . . . the rose—he remembered
giving each its name, remembered the green river, the shy,
green girl. He could no longer remember why it was he had
felt compelled to leave it except that it had something to do
with asserting his independence. Beyond that, he had only
the dim sense that somehow a terrible injustice had been
done, or possibly a terrible justice.

He saw the flame of what must have been the sunset flash
like a sword in the upper story windows across the street.
When the old steward brought him his third martini, he
called him Pete. Actually, his name was Angelo.

(Genesis 2–3)

AGAG

According to the prophet Samuel, God wanted King Saul
to wipe out every last one of the Amalekites—not just the
men but the women and children, the babies, the Old Folks
Home. When he heard that Saul had decided to spare the
Amalekite king, Agag, he was so enraged that he tore the
royal robe from Saul's back and told him to consider it a mild
foretaste of how God would tear the kingdom of Israel from
him next. He then had them drag out poor Agag, who was

quick to size up the situation. With something less than total conviction, he said, "Surely the bitterness of death is past" (1 Samuel 15:32). Within seconds Samuel had personally hacked him to pieces to prove that God meant what Samuel said that he said.

Since Agag had hacked quite a few people to pieces himself in his day, he may well have been dismayed by the experience but can hardly have been surprised. What was perhaps new to him was the length to which the friends of God will go to make God enemies.

(1 Samuel 15)

AGRIPPA

There's something a little sad about seeing anybody for the last time, even somebody you were never particularly crazy about to begin with. Agrippa, for instance. He was the last of the Herods (*see* HEROD ANTIPAS, HEROD THE GREAT), and after him that rather unsavory dynasty came to an end.

When Saint Paul was on his way to Rome to stand trial (*see* FELIX), King Agrippa granted him a preliminary hearing, and Paul, who was seldom at a loss for words, put up a strong defense. He described how on the road to Damascus he had come to believe Jesus was the Messiah (*see* PAUL) and how all he had been doing since was trying to persuade other people to believe he was right. He said the fact the Jews were out to get him showed only that they didn't understand their own scriptures because the whole thing was right there including the prediction that the Messiah would suffer and rise from the dead just the way Jesus had.

After he finished, Agrippa came out with the only remark he ever made that has gone down in history. "Almost thou persuadest me to become a Christian," he said (Acts 26:28).

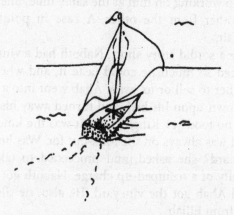

Almost is apt to be a sad word under the best of circumstances, and here, on the lips of the last of his line the last time you see him, it has a special poignance. If only Paul had been a little more eloquent. If only Agrippa had been a little more receptive, a little braver, a little crazier. If only God weren't such a stickler for letting people make up their own minds without coercing them. But things are what they are, and *almost* is the closest Agrippa ever got to what might have changed his life. It's sad enough to miss the boat at all, but to miss it by inches, with a saint right there to hand you aboard, is sadder still.

(Acts 26:1–28 King James Version)

AHAB

Whereas just about everybody has a cross to bear, King Ahab had two. One cross was the prophet Elijah. If, generally speaking, a prophet to a king was like ants at a picnic, Elijah was like a swarm of bees. The other cross was his foreign-born wife, Jezebel, who had gotten religion in a big way back in the old country and was forever trying to palm it off on the Israelites, who had a perfectly good religion of their own. Unfortunately for Ahab, the two of them sometimes got to working on him at the same time, one from one side, the other from the other. A case in point was the Naboth affair.

To make a sordid story short, Naboth had a vineyard that Ahab wanted so much he could taste it, and when Naboth refused either to sell or to swap, Ahab went into a sulk. "He laid him down upon his bed, and turned away his face, and would eat no food" (1 Kings 21:4). It was the kind of opening Jezebel was always on the look-out for. Was he a king or a cup custard? she asked, and proceeded to take charge. Found guilty of a trumped-up charge, Naboth got stoned to death, and Ahab got the vineyard. He also, needless to say, got a visit from Elijah.

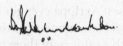

Down through the years they'd kept meeting like that, usually in secluded places, always at critical moments. Ahab arrived incognito—the dark glasses, the Panama hat, the business suit—and Elijah with a ten-day growth of beard. Ahab addressed him in his usual informal way as a royal pain in the neck (1 Kings 21:20), and then Elijah let him have it with both barrels. When God got through with him, Elijah said, there wouldn't be enough left of Ahab to scrape off the sidewalk, and what there was the dogs would take care of. As for Jezebel, not only because of Naboth but because of all her imported witch doctors and totem poles, she would end up the same way.

Ahab at least said he was sorry, and as a result was allowed to die honorably in battle, the part about the dogs coming true only in the sense that they got to lap the water up that his bloody chariot was hosed off with afterwards. Jezebel, on the other hand, continued unrepentant to the end. When the time finally came, they threw her out of the window, and when the dogs got finished, all that was left for the undertaker was "the skull and the feet and the palms of her hands" (2 Kings 9:35).

God is merciful, and if Jezebel and Ahab and Elijah all eventually met up again in Paradise, you can only assume that Ahab said if it weren't for the honor of the thing, he'd as soon take his chances in a warmer climate, and immediately put in for a transfer.

(1 Kings 21–22, 2 Kings 9:30–36)

AHASUERUS (See XERXES)

AMOS

When the prophet Amos walked down the main drag, it was like a shoot-out in the Old West. Everybody ran for cover. His special target was The Beautiful People, and

shooting from the hip, he never missed his mark. He pictures them sleek and tanned at Palm Beach, Acapulco, St. Tropez. They glisten with Bain de Soleil. The stereo is piped out over the marble terrace. Another tray of bloody Marys is on the way. A vacationing bishop plunges into the heated pool.

With one eye cocked on them, he has his other cocked on The Unbeautiful People—the varicose veins of the old waiter, the pasty face of the starch-fed child, the Indian winos passed out on the railroad siding, the ragged woman fumbling for food stamps at the check-out counter.

When justice is finally done, Amos says, there will be Hell to pay. The Happy Hour will be postponed indefinitely because the sun will never make it over the yard-arm. The Pucci blouses, the tangerine-colored slacks, the flowered Lillys, will all fade like grass. Nothing but a few chicken bones will mark the place where once the cold buffet was spread out under the royal palms.

But according to Amos, it won't be the shortage of food and fun that will hurt. It will be the shortage "of hearing the words of the Lord" (Amos 8:11). Towards the end, God will make himself so scarce that the world won't even know what it's starving to death for.

(Amos 6–8)

ANANIAS

It wasn't because Ananias held back from the poor box some of the proceeds of his real estate deal that Saint Peter came down on him so hard. The poor would get by somehow. They always had. What got the old saint's goat was that Ananias let on he was handing over his whole pile instead of only as much as he thought he wouldn't be needing himself.

"You have not lied to men but to God," Peter said (Acts 5:4), and the undeniable truth of the charge together with the unbearable shame of it were more than Ananias could take, so he dropped dead. His wife, Sapphira, had been in on

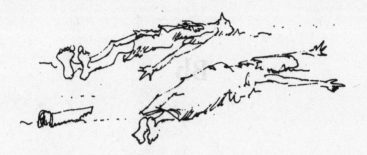

the real estate deal with him, and when she turned up three hours later and found out what had happened, she dropped dead too.

Lying to God is like sawing the branch you're sitting on. The better you do it, the harder you fall.

(Acts 5:1–11)

Bb

BALAAM

The legend of Solomon's ring, the adventures of Dr. Doolittle, the attempt to decipher the dots and dashes of dolphins and to teach chimpanzees to type out their thoughts on computers all reflect man's ancient dream of being able to talk with the animals. As fascinating as a message from outer space would be a message from the inner space of a great blue heron or a common house cat sunning herself on the kitchen linoleum. Their mute gaze suggests a vision of reality beyond our imagining. What do they see in their ignorance that we in our wisdom are mostly blind to?

In the Book of Numbers, Balaam's ass sees an angel of the Lord barring the way with a drawn sword in his hand and thereupon lies down in the middle of the road with Balaam still on his back. When Balaam clobbers him over the head with a stick, the ass speaks out reproachfully in fluent Hebrew, and then Balaam sees the angel too.

This is perhaps a clue to the mystery. Whereas men as a rule see only what they expect to see and little more, the animals, innocent of expectation, see what is there. The next time the old mare looks up from her browsing and lets fly with an exultant whinny at the empty horizon, we might do well to consider at least the possibility that the horizon may not be quite as empty as we think.

(Numbers 22:22–31)

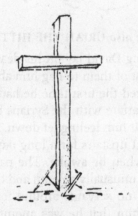

BARABBAS

Pilate told the people that they could choose to spare the life of either a murderer named Barabbas or Jesus of Nazareth, and they chose Barabbas. Given the same choice, Jesus, of course, would have chosen to spare Barabbas, too.

To understand the reason in each case would be to understand much of what the New Testament means by saying that Jesus is the Savior, and much of what it means too by saying that, by and large, people are in bad need of being saved.

(Mark 15:6–15)

BATHSHEBA (*See also* URIAH THE HITTITE)

Even when King David lay on his death-bed and she was there with the rest of them to nag him about the succession, he still remembered the first time he had ever seen her. The latest round of warfare with the Syrians had just ended, and his victory had left him feeling let down. He drank too much at lunch and went upstairs for a long nap afterwards. It was almost twilight when he awoke. The palace was unusually quiet, and he felt unusually solemn and quiet inside his own skin. There were no servants around for some reason, nobody to remind him that he was anointed king, victorious general, all that. He bathed, made himself a drink, and with just a towel wrapped around his waist, walked out onto the terrace on the roof where he looked down over the parapet in a kind of trance.

If the whole Syrian army had been drawn up in battle dress, he would have simply noted their presence and passed on. There was a bay gelding tethered to a tree, sweeping the flies away with his tail. In the servants' court, a cistern had overflowed onto the cobbles leaving a puddle the shape of Asia. Beyond a wall, a naked girl stood in a shallow pool dipping water over her shoulders with a shell. In as detached a way as he saw the girl, he saw both that he had to have her at any cost and that the cost would be exorbitant. Her husband's murder, the death of their first child—like actors awaiting their cues, the fatal consequences lurked just out of sight in the wings.

Years later, when the chill was in his bones and rattling with beads Bathsheba came to pester him about Solomon, he could hardly see her there at his bedside but saw her instead glimmering in the dusk like a peeled pear as he'd first gazed down at her from the roof with his glass in his hand all those years earlier. Raising it first to eye level, he had drained it off in a single swallow like a toast, but it was only on his deathbed that he caught a glimpse of why.

It wasn't just Bathsheba that he'd been toasting or the prospect of their life together but a much more distant prospect still. He had been drinking, he realized, to the child of their child of their child a thousand years thence who he could only pray would find it in his heart to think kindly someday of the beautiful girl and the improvident king who had so recklessly and long ago been responsible for his birth in a stable and his death just outside the city walls.

(2 Samuel 11–12)

BELSHAZZAR

There were blocks of ice carved into peacocks, gods, galleons in full sail. There were mounds of peeled shrimp and caviar, whole lambs roasted with their forepaws crossed like crusaders, suckling pigs cradled in lilies-of-the-valley and watercress. There were doves of whipped cream and meringue, a huge silver cake in the shape of a five-pointed star. Dwarfs and Nubians waited on a thousand guests. The sound of cymbals shivered across the teak floor where a sixteen-year-old virgin disported herself with a Barbary ape while the flames from basins of scented oil threw their shadows on the whitewashed walls of Belshazzar's palace.

It was all for the Persian ambassadors, who sat there with their absurd bonnets and their beards stiff with pomade. Belshazzar tried to read some clue to their secret thoughts in their little wedge-shaped smiles, but the smiles were as hard to decipher as their cuneiform inscriptions. He hadn't had a decent sleep for a week. His head was splitting. One of the eunuchs was nickering behind him like a mare in heat.

When the handwriting started to appear on the flame-lit wall, most people thought it was more of the floor show, and when Belshazzar offered an extravagant reward to anyone who could translate it properly, several senior ministers proposed various comic obscenities before they saw the king was serious as death. So finally he had them summon Daniel (q.v.), his late father's pet Jew and an expert on evil omens.

Daniel pointed out that among other things, the tables were laden with sacred vessels that had been looted from the Temple in Jerusalem. Some of them were clogged with cigarette butts. A big golden one inscribed with a name too holy to be spoken had been used by a concubine who had made herself sick on too much shrimp. A magenta-wigged creature of indeterminate sex was wearing another as a hat.

Like worshiping gods made of wood and stone, Daniel said, all this was another example of Belshazzar's fatal habit of getting the sacred and the profane hopelessly confused. Pointing to the ice-carved idols whose faces had already started running down their shirtfronts, Daniel said that what the handwriting on the wall meant in a nutshell was: The Party Is Over.

Sure enough, that very night, not long after the last guest had staggered home, Belshazzar was stabbed to death in sight of the Persian ambassadors with their wedge-shaped smiles, and just as the dwarfs were leading the exhausted ape home, Darius the Great, King of Persia, took Belshazzar's Babylon the way Grant took Richmond.

(Daniel 5)

BOAZ (*See* RUTH)

Cc

CAESAR AUGUSTUS

Caesar was only one of the titles Augustus bore. Others were *rex, imperator, princeps, pontifex maximus,* and so on. He ruled Rome and thus virtually the whole civilized world. He was worshiped as a god. People burned incense to him. Insofar as he is remembered at all, most people remember him mainly because at some point during his reign, in a rundown section of one of the more obscure imperial provinces, out behind a cheesy motel among cowflops and moldy hay, a child was born to a pair of up-country rubes you could have sold the Brooklyn Bridge to without even trying.

(Luke 2:1)

CAIAPHAS

The high priest Caiaphas was essentially a mathematician. When the Jews started worrying that they might all get into

20

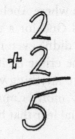

When he asked Cain where Abel was, Cain said, "How should I know? Am I supposed to keep an eye on him all the time?" but he knew the answer well enough. God knew it too, and because he loved Cain even with his brother's blood still moist on the grass, God decided to put a tribute on him and sentenced him to be a homeless tramp for the rest of his life, but to keep anybody from taking advantage of his fugitive status to bump him off, God put a special mark on his forehead to protect him.

hot water with the Romans because of the way Jesus was carrying on, Caiaphas said that in that case they should dump him like a hot potato. His argument ran that it is better for one man to get it in the neck for the sake of many than for many to get it in the neck for the sake of one man. His grim arithmetic proved unassailable.

The arithmetic of Jesus, on the other hand, was atrocious. He said that Heaven gets a bigger kick out of one sinner who repents than out of ninety-nine saints who don't need to. He said that God pays as much for one hour's work as for one day's. He said that the more you give away, the more you have.

It is curious that in the matter of deciding his own fate, he reached the same conclusion as Caiaphas and took it in the neck for the sake of many, Caiaphas included. It was not, however, the laws of mathematics that he was following.

(John 11:47–50)

CAIN

Abel was like his sheep—the same flat, complacent gaze, the thick curls low on the forehead, a voice like the creak of new shoes when he prayed. The prayers were invariably answered. His flocks fattened, and the wool fetched top price. His warts disappeared overnight. His advice to his brother Cain was invariably excellent. Cain took it about as long as he could and then let him have it with his pitchfork one afternoon while they were out tedding hay.

When God asked Cain where Abel was, Cain said, "I don't know," which didn't fool God for a minute, and "Am I my brother's keeper?" which didn't even rate an answer (Genesis 4:9). Even so, God let the crime be its own punishment instead of trying to think up anything worse: with no stomach for haying that field any more, Cain took up traveling instead but lived in continual fear that he'd be spotted as a fratricide and lynched.

When he complained to God about this, God gave him some kind of severe facial twitch which marked him as the sort of man you don't kick because he's down already and thus ensured him a long life in which to remember that last incredulous bleat, the glazing over of that flat, complacent gaze. The justice and mercy of God have seldom been so artfully combined in a single act.

(Genesis 4:1–16)

Dd

DANIEL (*See also* **SUSANNA**)

Nebuchadnezzar (q.v.) was in such a state when Daniel arrived at about four in the morning with a raincoat thrown over his pajamas that all the customary grovelings and mumbo-jumbo were dispensed with, and he received him the way any man might receive another at that hour—any man, that is, who'd just been scared out of his wits. The guards with their leash of panthers were dismissed, the slatted ivory blinds were pulled shut, and sitting bolt upright in the middle of his bed with the covers clutched in a knot at his throat, the king stammered out his appalling dream.

He said there was this enormous tree so heavy with leaves and fruit that it gave shade for miles around and all the beasts of the field came to take their ease in it.

"That's you," Daniel said.

He said there was this creature who came down from Heaven bearing orders that the tree was to be chopped down, its branches lopped off, and all its leaves and fruit scattered.

"I guess you know where those orders came from," Daniel said.

He said the mutilated stump that was left had its heart changed to a beast's heart, and the beast ate grass with oxen, and its hair got all matted like feathers, and its nails grew long and yellow like an owl's.

"That's to help you get back in touch with reality," Daniel said. "You've gotten so used to being treated like a God, you've started believing you are one."

When the thing finally happened, everybody was very tactful. Nebuchadnezzar would come grazing across the lawn on all fours, and they'd look the other way. He'd lift his leg on the marble balustrade, and business would go on as usual. He'd squat out there in the hanging gardens howling into the dusk as naked as the day he was born, but from everybody's polite expressions, you would have thought it was just the court musicians tuning up for the evening dinner-dance.

He was still lying out there on the grass one morning when the sun started to come up, and by the time it had cleared the tops of the tallest palms, he was back on two feet again and behaving quite normally. The way he explained it was that as he'd lain there watching the golden rays fan out across the sky, he'd suddenly realized that even a great king like himself must look pretty cheap compared with a God who could put on a show like that once a day and kept putting it on whether the audience was worth it or not because that was the kind of God he was.

"Now you're starting to talk sense," Daniel said.

It wasn't long after this that Nebuchadnezzar got back to the office again, full time, with Daniel as his right-hand man.

Except for a certain uneasiness in the presence of ruminants and an occasional friendly chat with his psychiatrist, it was comparatively clear sailing from there on out.

(Daniel 4)

DAVID (See also ABISHAG, ABSALOM, BATHSHEBA, GOLIATH, JONATHAN, MEPHIBOSHETH, NATHAN, RUTH, SAUL)

To see what there was about David that made Israel adore him like no other king she ever had, as good a place to look as any is the account of how he captured Jerusalem and moved in the ark.

Jerusalem was a major plum for the new young king, a hill town considered so untakeable that the inhabitants had a saying to the effect that a blind man and a cripple could hold it against the U.S. Marines (2 Samuel 5:6). Just to remind people who it was that had nevertheless finally taken it, David's first move was to change its name to the City of David. His second move was a brilliant maneuver for giving his victory the stamp of divine approval by trotting out that holy box of acacia wood overlaid with gold which was known as the ark and contained who knows what but was as close as Israel ever officially got to a representation in space of their God who dwelled in eternity. David had the ark loaded onto a custom-built cart and made a regular circus parade of it, complete with horns, harps, cymbals, and psalteries, not to mention himself high-stepping out front like the Mayor of Dublin on Saint Patrick's Day. When they finally made it into town, he set up a big tent to keep out the weather, had refreshments passed around on the house, and, just so nobody would forget who was picking up the tab, did the lion's share of the praying himself and personally took up the collection afterwards.

So far it was none of it anything a good public relations man couldn't have dreamed up for him, but the next thing was something else again. He stripped down to his skivvies, and then with everybody looking on including his wife—a high-class girl named Michal who gave his administration tone as the late King Saul's daughter—he did a dance. Maybe it started out as just another Madison Avenue ploy, but not for long.

With trumpets blaring and drums beating, it was Camelot all over again, and for once that royal young red-head didn't have to talk up the bright future and the high hopes because he was himself the future at its brightest, and there were no hopes higher than the ones his people had in him. And for once he didn't have to drag God in for politics' sake either because it was obvious to everybody that this time God was there on his own. How they cut loose together, David and Yahweh, whirling around before the ark in such a passion that they caught fire from each other and blazed up in a single flame of such magnificence that not even the dressing-down David got from Michal afterwards could dim the glory of it.

He had feet of clay like the rest of us if not more so—self-serving and deceitful, lustful and vain—but on the basis of that dance alone, you can see why it was David more than anybody else that Israel lost her heart to and why, when Jesus of Nazareth came riding into Jerusalem on his flea-bitten mule a thousand years later, it was as the Son of David that they hailed him.

(2 Samuel 5–6)

DEBORAH (See also JAEL)

Deborah was Israel's only woman judge. She looked like Golda Meir and did business under a palm tree. Her business consisted of more than just stepping in and settling things when people got in a wrangle. Like all the other judges of Israel, she was loaded with charisma, and whenever there was any fighting to be done, she was the one who was in charge. Even generals jumped when she snapped her fingers. Barak, for instance.

She summoned him to the palm tree and told him she wanted him to take ten thousand of his best men and beat the stuffing out of the Canaanite forces under a general named Sisera. Barak said he'd do it but indicated he'd feel more secure if Deborah came along. She said she would. She also said it was only fair to warn him, however, that the main glory of the day was going to be not his but a woman's because a woman was going to be the one to wipe out Sisera. In addition to her other hats, Deborah was also something of a prophet and had pronounced feminist sympathies.

Her prediction turned out to be correct, of course. Barak won the battle, but Sisera was disposed of by a lady named Jael (q.v.) in a rather spectacular way that can be read about in the proper place, and to make sure that Jael got all the credit that was coming to her, Deborah wrote a song to help spread the word around.

It is a wonderful song, full of blood and thunder with a lot of hair-raisingly bitter jibes at the end of it about how Sisera's old mother sits waiting at the window for her son to come home, not knowing that Jael has already made mincemeat of him. Deborah composed it, but she got Barak to sing it with her. Barak looked like Moshe Dayan, and it must have been quite a duet. The song brushes by Barak's role rather hastily, but it describes Jael's in lavish detail and must have gotten her all the glory a girl could possibly want. Yahweh himself gets a plug at the end—"So perish all thine enemies, O Lord!" (Judges 5:31)—but by and large the real hero of Deborah's song is herself. Everything was going to pot, the lyrics say, "until you arose, Deborah, arose as a mother in Israel" (Judges 5:7), and you can't help feeling that Deborah's basic message was that Mother was the one who really saved the day. And of course, with Yahweh's help, she was.

It's hard not to bridle a little at the idea of her standing under the palm tree belting out her own praises like that, but after all, she had a country to run and a war to fight, and she knew that without a good press she was licked from the start. Besides, maybe the more self-congratulatory parts of her song were the ones that she assigned to Barak.

(Judges 4–5)

DELILAH

She knew from the start that all she had to do to ruin Samson was cut off his gorgeous mop. It wasn't for nothing that she'd lain in bed watching him brush it in the mirror like a girl, the self-conscious way he tossed it out of his eyes on the dance floor, the silk bandana he tied it back with when he went gunning for Philistines. It was only to give them a few more days together that she pretended to swallow his clumsy fibs about how the way to get the better of him was with new rope, bowstrings, and so on.

But Philistine Headquarters got tough with her finally, so one night when he was asleep with his head in her lap, she slipped out her scissors, and by the time she was through with him, he looked like Mr. Clean. Even the Philistine goon squad had some qualms about jumping a man who was crying like a baby when they came in to get him, and after the look she saw him give his reflection in the dresser mirror as they dragged him out, she had the feeling that it was almost a relief to him when they put out his eyes.

(Judges 16)

DINAH

Everybody agreed that Jacob's daughter Dinah had something special about her.

She was off visiting friends in Canaan when young Shechem the Hivite was so dazzled that he couldn't control himself and took advantage of her. Considering the degree of the temptation, you could hardly blame him in a way, but when Dinah's brothers got wind of it, they hit the roof.

Shechem by this time had fallen head over heels in love, but even when he wanted to make an honest woman of her and came to beg Jacob for her hand in marriage, the brothers were not mollified. On the contrary, they felt that he was only adding insult to injury.

Shechem would not take no for an answer. He said that if Jacob would give his permission, he would make it worth his while by arranging some advantageous trade agreements between their two tribes with some personal gifts of cash and real estate thrown in for good measure. It was the kind of offer Jacob always found hard to refuse, but at the urging of his sons, he agreed to make one more condition.

If Shechem wanted to marry a nice Jewish girl like Dinah, he said, then he and all his fellow tribesmen would have to get themselves circumcised. It was the custom. Shechem didn't find it the easiest thing in the world to sell his fellow tribesmen, but somehow he managed it, and that was the break Dinah's brothers had been waiting for.

While the Hivites were still recovering from surgery, the brothers appeared out of nowhere and mowed them down to the last Hivite. When Jacob chided them about it afterwards, they seemed quite nonplussed. For Dinah's sake, who would have done less?

Dinah herself had done nothing except be who she was, which was the kind of person men naturally want to die for or kill for, but that was enough. "Terrible as an army with banners" is the way Solomon describes beauty in his *Song,* and you picture her standing there with downcast eyes before her brothers' butchery, totally innocent of the knowledge that there were glittering battalions in her mildest smile and that if she wanted to take the world on single-handed, the world wouldn't stand a chance.

(Genesis 34)

Ee

ELIJAH (*See also* AHAB)

In the contest between Elijah and the prophets of Baal to see whose God was the real article, Elijah won the first round hands down. Starting out early in the morning on Mt. Carmel, the prophets of Baal pulled out all the stops to get their candidate to set fire to the sacrificial offering. They danced around the altar till their feet were sore. They made themselves hoarse shouting instructions and encouragement at the sky. They jabbed at themselves with knives thinking that the sight of blood would start things moving if anything would, but they might as well have saved themselves the trouble.

Although it was like beating a dead horse, Elijah couldn't resist getting in a few digs. "Maybe Baal's flown to Bermuda for the weekend," he said. "Maybe he's taking a nap." The prophets whipped themselves into greater and greater frenzies under his goading, but by mid-afternoon the sacrificial offering had begun to smell a little high, and there was still no sign of fire from above. Then it was Elijah's turn to show what Yahweh could do.

He was like a magician getting ready to pull a rabbit out of a hat. First he had a trench dug around the altar and filled with water. Then he got a bucket brigade going to give the offering a good dowsing too. Then as soon as they'd finished, he got them to do it again for good measure. By the time they'd finished a third go-round, the whole place was awash, and Elijah looked as if he'd just finished swimming the channel. He then gave Yahweh the word to show his stuff and jumped back just in time.

Lightning flashed. The water in the trench fizzed like fat on a hot griddle. Nothing was left of the offering but a pile of ashes and a smell like the Fourth of July. The onlookers were beside themselves with enthusiasm and at a signal from Elijah demolished the losing team down to the last prophet. Nobody could say whose victory had been greater, Yahweh's or Elijah's.

But the sequel to the event seems to have made this clear. Queen Jezebel (see AHAB) was determined to get even with Elijah for what he had done to her spiritual advisers, and to save his skin he went and hid out on Mt. Horeb. Again he gave Yahweh the word, not because he wanted anything set on fire this time but just to keep his hand in.

Again the lightning flashed, and after that a wind came up that almost blew Elijah off his feet, and after that the earth gave such a shake that it almost knocked him silly. But there wasn't so much as a peep out of Yahweh, and Elijah stood there like a ringmaster when the lion won't jump through the hoop.

Only when the fireworks were finished and a terrible hush fell over the mountain did Elijah hear something, and what he heard was so much like silence that it was only through the ear of faith that he knew it was Yahweh. Nonetheless, the message came through loud and clear: that there was no longer any question who had been the star at Mt. Carmel and that not even Elijah could make the Lord God of Hosts jump through a hoop like a lion or pop out like a rabbit from a hat.

(1 Kings 18–19)

ELISHA (*See also* NAAMAN)

It was a hot day as the prophet Elisha made his way up to Bethel where he had business to attend to. Pausing near a camping ground for a bit of shade, he was mopping his bald scalp with a corner of his prayer shawl when a boy scout troop broke ranks and surrounded him. They threw bottle caps at him, and they made rude gestures. They pulled their mouths out as wide as they could with their thumbs and at the same time pulled their lower lids down with their index fingers till you could see the wet, pink membrane inside. It was an unnerving spectacle.

"Skin-head" and "Chrome-dome" and "Curly" they called at him till finally the old man had enough. He made a few passes at them, muttered a few words, and within seconds a couple of she-bears lumbered out from the trees behind the picnic tables and mauled some of the slower members of the troop rather badly.

It is not the most edifying story in the Old Testament, but there are perhaps some lessons to be learned from it even so. The Lord does not call everyone to be Mister Rogers, for instance, and there is no need to try making a fool out of a prophet because sooner or later he will probably make one out of himself. It is not the most edifying story about Elisha either, but it is perhaps one of the more endearing.

(2 Kings 2:23–25)

ESAU

Esau was so hungry he could hardly see straight when his younger twin, Jacob, bought his birthright for a bowl of chili. He was off hunting rabbits when Jacob conned their old father, Isaac, into giving him the blessing that should have been Esau's by right of primogeniture. Eventually it dawned on Esau what his brother was up to and he went slogging after him with a blunt instrument; but the slowness of his wits was compensated for by the generosity of his disposition, and in time the two were reconciled.

Jacob stole Esau blind, in other words, got away with it, and went on to become the father of the twelve tribes of Israel. It was not all gravy, however. He knew famine and loss.

He grieved for years over the supposed death of his favorite child. He was as hoodwinked by his own sons in this as both his father and Esau had been hoodwinked by him, and he died with the clamor of their squabbling shrill in his ears.

Esau, on the other hand, though he'd lost his shirt, settled down in the hill country, raised a large if comparatively undistinguished family, and died in peace. Thus it seems hard to know which of the two brothers came out ahead in the end.

It seems plain enough, however, that the reason God by-passed Esau and made Jacob heir to the great promise is that it is easier to make a silk purse out of a sow's ear than out of a dim bulb.

(Genesis 25–27, 33)

ESTHER (*See* XERXES)

ETHIOPIAN EUNUCH

His name isn't given, but he was Secretary of the Treasury under Queen Candace of Ethiopia, and he had been to Jerusalem on a religious pilgrimage. It was on his way home that the high point of the trip occurred.

He was cruising along in his chariot reading out loud to himself from the Book of Isaiah when the apostle Philip hap-

pened to overhear him and asked if he understood what the words were all about. The eunuch said he could use some help on one passage in particular, and this was the passage:

> As a sheep led to the slaughter
>   or a lamb before its shearers is dumb
> so he opens not his mouth.
> In his humiliation justice was denied him.
> Who can describe his generation?
> For his life is taken up from the earth.
>
> (Acts 8:32–33, compare Isaiah 53:7–8)

Who in the world was Isaiah talking about? the eunuch wanted to know, and Philip said it was Jesus. Jesus was the one who was gentle as a sheep and innocent as a lamb. He was the one who had been unjustly humiliated and slaughtered and hadn't let out so much as a peep to save himself. As for describing his generation, his time, all you could say was that he belonged to all time and every generation because his life wasn't bound to the earth any more. His life was everywhere, and anybody could live it for himself or let it live itself in him as easily as a fish circulates around in the water and the water circulates around in a fish.

The way things happened, a pond turned up by the side of the road as they traveled along, and the eunuch said why shouldn't he give the thing a try right then and there and let Philip baptize him in it? So Philip baptized him, and when that black and mutilated potentate bobbed back to the surface, he was so carried away he couldn't even speak. The sounds of his joy were like the sounds of a brook rattling over pebbles, and Philip never saw him again and never had to.

> (Acts 8:26–39)

EUTYCHUS

"Sermonettes make Christianettes," the saying goes, so Saint Paul kept talking till midnight to make sure they all got the word. Then he thought of a few things he'd left out and went on a while longer. He was so caught up in his own eloquence that he didn't hear the bumblebee sounds that were emerging from a young man with his eyes more or less closed and his mouth more or less open who sat slumped over in the third story window. It was only a woman's scream that alerted him to the fact that the boy had fallen asleep, and out, more or less simultaneously. When Paul asked his name, they told him it was Eutychus.

Everybody thought Eutychus was dead, but Paul said he'd see about that. Then he went back upstairs where, after a snack, he ran over his major points once more just to make sure. When he finally left on the early bus, they found Eutychus sitting up in bed asking for two over light and a toasted English.

This miraculous recovery, plus the fact that by then the saint was already well on his way to the next county, made them decide to throw a double celebration. Presumably somebody had the sense to suggest that this time they use the ground floor.

(Acts 20:9–12)

EVE (*See also* ADAM)

Like Adam, she spent the rest of her days convincing herself that it had all worked out for the best. Their new life didn't turn out to be as bad as had been predicted, and somehow their marriage weathered the change. If they had moments of terrible bitterness over what had happened, they had other moments when it became more of a bridge than an abyss between them and when the question of which of them was to blame got lost in the question of how both of them were to survive. One son died an ugly, senseless death, and another went through life as disfigured by remorse as by a cleft palate (*see* CAIN). But all in all things didn't go too badly. When the last child left home, it wasn't the easiest thing in the world to be alone again with a man who after his third martini might still lash out at her as a snake in the grass and a bad apple, but at least they still had their independence and their principles, which as nearly as she could remember were what they'd given everything up for. They stood, however grimly at times, on their own feet.

It was only once in a while at night, just as she was going off to sleep with all her usual defenses down, that her mind drifted back to the days when, because there was nothing especially important to do, everything was especially important; when *too good not to be true* hadn't yet turned into *too good to be true*; when being alone was never the same as being lonely. Then sad and beautiful dreams overtook her which she would wake up from homesick for a home she could no longer even name, to make something not quite love with a man whose face she could not quite see in the darkness at her side.

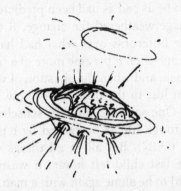

(Genesis 3:1–4:16)

EZEKIEL

A popular view has it that what Ezekiel really saw was flying saucers.

There were these gleaming wheels with spokes and rims and things that looked like eyes built into the rims, he said, and one minute they were resting on the ground, and the next minute they were shooting up into the sky. There were also these creatures who flew around with the wheels and made a noise like thunder or a sonic boom, he said. Above them was this one creature in particular who looked humanoid but was clearly not human and seemed to be wearing something like bronze or a space-suit from the loins up and something like fire from the loins down.

Then all of a sudden from way up in the air his voice came down, and all the other craft stopped shooting around and just hovered, and to make a long story from outerspace short, what the voice said was that if Israel didn't whip itself into some kind of shape, it would be curtains.

Ezekiel didn't think he'd seen flying saucers, of course. He thought he'd seen the glory of God. And the close encounter he thought he'd had wasn't of the third kind but of a different kind altogether. It wasn't a thirty-foot praying mantis he thought had given him the word but the Almighty himself.

So you pay your money and take your choice.

In making that choice, however, you ought to take into consideration at least one other thing Ezekiel thought he saw. It was a bone-yard. There were shin bones and arm bones and wish bones and collar bones and skulls enough to keep paleontologists busy indefinitely. What the voice said this time was for Ezekiel to speak the word of the Lord to this bone yard and then stand back. So he spoke it.

The first thing that happened was a sound of rattling and clicking like the tide going out over a million pebble beaches as the bones started snapping back together again. The next thing that happened was a million reassembled skeletons pulling on skin like long winter underwear. The last thing that happened was the color coming back to a million pairs of cheeks and the spark to a million pairs of eyes and the breath of life to a million pairs of lungs.

Then the voice asked Ezekiel to tell Israel that—with God in the wings—even though it would be curtains for sure the way they were heading, the curtain that goes down when you bomb in New Haven is also the curtain that goes up on the marvelous new rewrite that hits Broadway like a ton of bricks.

As far as is known, nobody's ever stepped out of a UFO and made a statement like that.

(Ezekiel 1–2:7, 37:1–14)

Ff

FELIX

Felix was the Roman governor of Cilicia. When Paul got into a knock-down drag-out with the Jerusalem Jews, Felix was the one that the Roman brass took him to in hopes of getting the matter settled once and for all. Paul's Roman passport entitled him to a Roman hearing, and Felix gave it to him. He seems to have listened sympathetically enough and to have had a fairly good understanding of both sides of the issue since on the one hand he already knew about the Christian movement and, on the other, he had a Jewish wife. Under the pretext of awaiting further evidence, he then placed Paul under custody but went out of the way to see to it that he was well taken care of. He could do what he wanted within reason, and his friends were allowed to supplement his rations from a kosher delicatessen.

The trouble came during a second interview a couple of days later. Felix had summoned him to find out how much his release was worth to him in hard cash, but with his usual tact Paul insisted on discussing justice, self-control, and future judgment instead. "Don't call me, I'll call you," Felix said and sent him back to the pokey. He dropped in on him there from time to time to pursue his original line of inquiry, but Paul never seemed to zero in on what he was after.

With three squares a day, a roof over his head, and plenty of time to write letters, Paul had no major complaints apparently, and as long as Felix didn't spring him, the Jews had no major complaints either. As for Felix himself, after two years he retired on a handsome government pension, leaving the problem of what to do with Paul for his successor to worry about. *Felix*, of course, means "the happy one" in Latin, and if happiness consists of having your cake and eating it too, he was well named.

(Acts 23:26–24:27)

Gg

GABRIEL

She struck the angel Gabriel as hardly old enough to have a child at all, let alone this child, but he'd been entrusted with a message to give her, and he gave it.

He told her what the child was to be named, and who he was to be, and something about the mystery that was to come upon her. "You mustn't be afraid, Mary," he said.

As he said it, he only hoped she wouldn't notice that beneath the great, golden wings he himself was trembling with fear to think that the whole future of creation hung now on the answer of a girl.

(Luke 1:26–35)

GEHAZI (*See* NAAMAN)

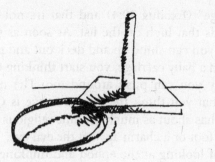

GIDEON

The best thing the judge Gideon ever did and the worst mistake he ever made came within moments of each other.

The best was when the Israelites asked him to be their king, and he turned down the invitation. Like the prophet Samuel years later (q.v.), he knew that the only true king Israel would ever have was Yahweh, and he told them so. If he had any secret hankerings for personal power, he managed to squelch them. It was a noble move, and when you consider all the trouble Israel had with kings when she finally got them, it showed amazing wisdom and foresight.

And then the mistake. All the boys were wearing gold earrings that season, and when Gideon asked them to contribute them to the cause, they cheerfully agreed. Somebody laid a coat on the ground, and as soon as the earrings were all tossed in, Gideon added some more golden gewgaws he'd taken from the enemy, things like crescents and pendants and collars for prize camels. By the time he was through, he had a great glittering pile out of which he made an ephod. Nobody's quite sure what an ephod was in this case, but it was apparently some sort of religious *objet d'art* that Gideon thought would remind everybody who their true king really was. Only that's not the way things worked out.

Gideon's mistake was to forget that the second of the Ten Commandments is "Thou shalt not make unto thee any graven image" (Exodus 20:4) and that it's not by accident that it stands that high on the list. As soon as you've got a golden god you can shine up and deck out and push around like a doll in a baby carriage, you start thinking God himself is somebody you can push around too. The next step, of course, is that you think the graven image is God, and by that time it has about as much genuine religious significance as a rabbit's foot or a charm against the evil eye.

Instead of looking at the ephod and thinking about Yahweh, the Israelites started kowtowing to the ephod and hardly giving Yahweh the time of day. After Gideon died, they started kowtowing to the kinds of things you win tossing hoops at a carnival, and Yahweh was all but forgotten.

Poor Gideon. He might almost have done better to let them make him king when they wanted to. At least he would have been able to keep them on the right track that way, and they would have been able to keep their earrings, and Yahweh would have been able to keep in closer touch with his people than for their many long, sad years of god-sampling was possible again.

(Judges 8:22–28)

GOLIATH

Goliath stood ten feet tall in his stocking feet, wore a size 20 collar, a 9½-inch hat, and a 52-inch belt. When he put his full armor on, he not only looked like a Sherman tank but weighed like one. Even stripped to the bare essentials, he had plenty to carry around, and flesh and bones were the least of it. There was the burdensome business of having to

defend his title against all comers. There were the mangled remains of the runners-up. When he tried to think something out, it was like struggling through a hip-deep bog. When he tried to explain something, it was like pushing a truck uphill. His dark moods were leaden and his light moods elephantine. He considered under-arm deodorants a sign of effeminacy.

The stone from David's slingshot caught him between the eyes, and when he hit the dirt, windows rattled in their frames as far away as Ashkelon. The ringing in his ears drowned out the cat-calls of the onlooking armies and his vision was all but shot, but he could still see enough to make out the naked figure of a boy running toward him through the scrub. His hair streamed out behind him like copper, and he was as swift and light-footed as a deer.

As he straddled Goliath with Goliath's sword in his hand, the giant believed that what he was seeing was his own soul stripped of the unwieldy flesh at last for its journey to Paradise, and when David presented the severed head to Saul later, there was an unmistakable smile on its great lips.

(1 Samuel 17:4–55)

GOMER

She was always good company—a little heavy with the lipstick maybe, a little less than choosy about men and booze, a little loud, but great at a party and always good for a laugh. Then the prophet Hosea came along wearing a sandwich board that read "The End Is at Hand" on one side and "Watch Out" on the other.

The first time he asked her to marry him, she thought he was kidding. The second time she knew he was serious but thought he was crazy. The third time she said yes. He wasn't exactly a swinger, but he had a kind face, and he was generous, and he wasn't all that crazier than everybody else. Besides, any fool could see he loved her.

Give or take a little, she even loved him back for a while, and they had three children whom Hosea named with queer names like Not-pitied-for-God-will-no-longer-pity-Israel-now-that-it's-gone-to-the-dogs so that every time the roll was called at school, Hosea would be scoring a prophetic bullseye in absentia. But everybody could see the marriage wasn't going to last, and it didn't.

While Hosea was off hitting the sawdust trail, Gomer took to hitting as many night spots as she could squeeze into a night, and any resemblance between her next batch of children and Hosea was purely coincidental. It almost killed him, of course. Every time he raised a hand to her, he burst into tears. Every time she raised one to him, he was the one who ended up apologizing.

He tried locking her out of the house a few times when she wasn't in by five in the morning, but he always opened the door when she finally showed up and helped get her to bed if she couldn't see straight enough to get there herself. Then one day she didn't show up at all.

He swore that this time he was through with her for keeps, but of course he wasn't. When he finally found her, she was lying passed out in a highly specialized establishment located above an adult bookstore, and he had to pay the management plenty to let her out of her contract. She'd lost her front teeth and picked up some scars you had to see to believe, but Hosea had her back again and that seemed to be all that mattered.

He changed his sandwich board to read "God Is Love" on one side and "There's No End to It" on the other, and when he stood on the street corner belting out

> How can I give you up, O Ephraim!
> How can I hand you over, O Israel!
> For I am God and not man,
> The Holy One in your midst.
>
> (Hosea 11:8–9)

nobody can say how many converts he made, but one thing that's for sure is that, including Gomer's, there was seldom a dry eye in the house.

(Hosea 1–3, 11)

Hh

HAGAR

Sarah couldn't have children so she persuaded her husband Abraham to have a child with her lady's maid Hagar instead. Abraham and Hagar both proved willing, and soon a child was on the way.

As you'd think one of them might have foreseen, however, there are certain problems inherent in a *ménage à trois* which are not solved by the prospect of its becoming a *ménage à quatre*. *Au contraire.*

As Sarah saw it, Hagar no longer walked around the house, she flounced, and whenever she had a craving for things like bagels and lox, naturally Abraham went out and got them for her. In no time at all Sarah was livid with jealousy. Eager for peace at any price, Abraham said to go ahead and fire Hagar then if that would make things better, and within a short time Hagar was out on the street with all her belongings piled around her including a layette.

It wasn't long, however, before an angel found her there and persuaded her to go back in and try to patch things up with her mistress. Not having anything better in mind, Hagar agreed. Then the angel told her that the Lord had taken pity on her and wanted her to know that she was to name her baby Ishmael when it came. He also wanted her to know that though Ishmael was never going to win any popularity contests, he would nonetheless be the first of a multitude of descendants. It was a promise. Much cheered by this, Hagar returned to the house through the servants' entrance, ate humble pie, and was eventually given back her old job. A few months later, Ishmael was born just as the Lord had said.

But her troubles weren't over. To the stupefaction of her gynecologists, it wasn't long before Sarah herself gave birth to a son named Isaac, who God promised would be the father of a great nation. This was so far beyond her wildest expectations, not to mention everybody else's, that for a while she was as happy as she'd ever been; but then one day she found Isaac and Ishmael playing together in the nursery, and once again the fat was in the fire.

She was convinced that her upstairs son would have to split his inheritance with Hagar's downstairs brat, so for the second time she nagged Abraham into driving them both out of the house permanently. When they got as far as Beersheba, they ran out of water. Hagar gave up her son for dead and sat down and wept.

It all ended happily, however. This time the Lord took care of her personally. First he produced a well and then he told her to dry her eyes because not only would her son live but he gave her his word that the boy would grow up to be the father of a great nation just like his half-brother Isaac back home. And so it came to pass.

The story of Hagar is the story of the terrible jealousy of Sarah and the singular ineffectuality of Abraham and the way Hagar, who knew how to roll with the punches, managed to survive them both. Above and beyond that, however, it is the story of how in the midst of the whole unseemly affair the Lord, half tipsy with compassion, went around making marvelous promises, and loving everybody, and creating great nations, like the last of the big-time spenders handing out hundred dollar bills.

(Genesis 16, 21)

HAM

Ham was the youngest of Noah's two sons and by tradition the progenitor of the black race.

After the Flood was over and the family had settled down into the wine business, Noah did a little too much sampling one hot afternoon and passed out buck naked in his tent. Ham happened to stick his head in at just the wrong moment and then, instead of keeping his mouth shut, went out and treated his brothers to a lurid account of what he'd seen.

When Noah sobered up and found out about it, he blew his top. Among some other unpleasant things he had to say was a curse to the effect that from that day forward Ham was to be his brothers' slave.

For generations certain preachers have pointed to this text as Biblical sanction for whatever form of white supremacy happened to be going on at the time all the way from literal slavery to separate but equal schools, segregated toilet facilities, and restricted housing.

"The Devil can cite Scripture for his purpose," says Shakespeare, and you can just see him standing up there with his paunch and his black robe citing it. As somebody once said, comparing the church to Noah's ark, if it weren't for the storm without, you could never stand the stench within.

(Genesis 9:18–27)

HAMAN (See XERXES)

HEROD ANTIPAS

Herod Antipas, the son of Herod the Great and the tetrarch of Galilee, seems to have spent much of his life running scared.

When John the Baptist started criticizing his private life in public, Herod had him locked up for fear that otherwise he might become a fad, but he didn't dare have him executed for fear that John's fans might get themselves a new tetrarch if he did.

On his birthday he told Salome that he'd give her anything she asked for if she'd do her act with the seven veils for him, and when what she asked for was John the Baptist's head on a platter, he shook in his boots but gave it to her because he was afraid of what might happen if word got around that he was turning chicken.

He turned pale when he heard that a new prophet named Jesus was stirring up trouble because he was sure that it

must be John come back from the grave to get even, and he decided to have him taken care of a second time. This threat doesn't seem to have especially bothered Jesus because when news of it reached him, he referred to Herod as a fox and sent word back that he had bigger things on his mind to worry about. (His use of the word *fox* is interesting because although then as now it could be used to suggest slyness, its more common use apparently was a term of contempt. *Pussy-cat* might be a better rendering. The fact that the Greek word is in the feminine gender may or may not be an allusion to some of Herod's more exotic proclivities.)

They finally came face to face, of course, Jesus of Nazareth and the tetrarch of Galilee. It was the night of Jesus's arrest, and when Pilate found out he was a Galilean and thus under that jurisdiction, he had him bundled off to Herod's head-quarters immediately. He'd never been able to stand Herod's guts, Luke tells us, and was probably tickled pink to find this way of needling him.

Ironically enough, it appears that Herod was tickled pink too because he'd apparently given up the idea that the man was John the Baptist's ghost and, again according to Luke, had been looking forward for a long time to seeing him perform some of his more spectacular tricks. He thought that if he was who they claimed he was, it should be quite a show. Unfortunately, Jesus refused to accommodate him or even to answer his questions, and taking this to be a sign of weakness, Herod decided to have a little fun with him.

He had his soldiers rough him up for a while and then let them do some other things to him that struck them as appropriate to do to a man who'd been the cause of their having been woken up in the middle of the night. When all of this was finished, Herod had them doll him up in one of his fanciest tetrarch uniforms with a few hilarious additions and deletions and in that state sent him back to Pilate.

As luck would have it, Pilate turned out to have the same sense of humor, and Luke tells us that he and Herod became great friends from then on. It is nice to think that at least one good thing thus came out of that dark and harrowing night, and it is interesting also to note that on this one occasion when Herod might justifiably have been scared out of his wits, you would have thought he was watching a Punch and Judy show the way he threw back his head and howled.

(Luke 13:31–35, 23:1–12, Matthew 14:1–12)

HEROD THE GREAT

The foolishness of the wise is perhaps nowhere better illustrated than by the way the three Magi went to Herod the Great, King of the Jews, to find out the whereabouts of the holy child who had just been born King of the Jews to supplant him. It did not even strike them as suspicious when Herod asked them to be sure to let him know when they found him so he could hurry on down to pay his respects.

Luckily for the holy child, after the three Magi had followed their star to the manger and left him their presents, they were tipped off in a dream to avoid Herod like the plague on their way home.

Herod was fit to be tied when he realized he'd been had and ordered the murder of every male child two years old and under in the district. For all his enormous power, he knew there was somebody in diapers more powerful still. The wisdom of the foolish is perhaps nowhere better illustrated.

(Matthew 2)

HIRAM

Hiram, King of Tyre, was in the lumber business, and when Solomon, King of Israel, decided he wanted to build the Temple in Jerusalem, Hiram let him have all the cedar and cypress he needed. He also charged such a cutthroat price for it that in order to pay up, Solomon had to tax his people blind and increase tolls on all the major highways.

Twenty years later, however, when the job was done and Hiram submitted his final bill, Solomon got a little of his own back by paying it in the form not of cash but of twelve Galilean cities whose turn-in value is suggested by the fact that when Hiram saw them, he called them Cabul, which means No Place. According to the historian Josephus,

Solomon followed this up by proposing a riddle contest which Hiram lost hands down. As a result he had to give Solomon an enormous prize.

Josephus reports that Hiram bided his time for a while but then got hold of a friend named Abdemon who made hash of Solomon's riddles in about twenty-five minutes, and at the end of that round it was Solomon who had to cough up an enormous prize for Hiram.

Unfortunately neither Josephus nor the Book of Kings reports what new heights the friendship rose to after that.

(1 Kings 5, 9)

HOLOFERNES (See JUDITH)

HOSEA (See GOMER)

Ii

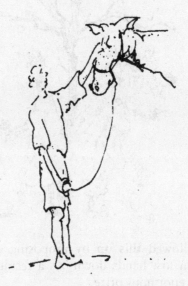

ISAAC (*See also* ESAU, HAGAR, JACOB, REBECCA)

With one possible exception, there has perhaps never been a birth more longed for and rejoiced in than Isaac's. Sarah was in her nineties when an angel told her that after years of barrenness she and her centenarian husband, Abraham, were finally going to have the child that God had promised them, and their wild and incredulous mirth at this news prompted them to name him Isaac, which in Hebrew means *laughter.* He is a shadowy figure compared to his father, Abraham, and his son Jacob, but at certain moments in his life the shadows recede about him, and he stands on the stage in a flood of light.

He was just a boy when, to see what Abraham was made of, God said that he was to take Isaac up into the hills and make a burnt offering of him. Abraham didn't have the heart to tell him what was going to happen, and if Isaac guessed, he didn't have the heart to admit that he did as they trudged side by side up the steep track. A mule was loaded down with the things they needed for making the fire, but the sacrificial animal was conspicuously absent, and when Isaac asked about it, Abraham choked out an evasive answer as best he could. By the time the wood was all laid out and ready to be lit, Isaac no longer had any doubts as to what lay in store for him, and maybe the reason he didn't fight for his life was that suddenly it didn't seem to him all that much worth fighting for. He let himself be tied up and laid out on top of the wood like an unblemished lamb, and, shaking like a leaf, the old man got as far as raising the knife over his head when God spoke up at last and said he'd seen all he needed to see and Isaac could use it on a ram instead. The lights switch off there, and the stage is returned mercifully to darkness.

Isaac was getting pretty long in the tooth himself when Abraham finally died, and he and his half brother Ishmael (see HAGAR) buried him in the same cave that years before Abraham had bought to bury Sarah in. If either of them said anything while they were at it, their words were not recorded, and maybe the scene was played out in silence—the two old men leaning on their shovels, out of breath, with the old man who had nearly been the end of both of them in his day lying six feet deep beneath their aching feet.

Isaac was on the verge of second childhood and almost blind when his son Jacob conned him into thinking he was his other son, Esau, so he could get the old man's blessing and the lion's share of the estate when that time came. Isaac had a hunch there was something fishy going on and called the young man over to be sure. The young man said he was

Esau, but it was in Jacob's voice that he said it. Isaac couldn't trust his hearing all that much better than his eyesight, however, so he told him to let him touch him with his hands. Esau's hands were hairy, and he knew he'd know them anywhere. But Jacob had seen that coming, and Isaac wasn't sure whether what he felt were Esau's hairy hands or a pair of bearskin gloves. In fact there was so little he could be sure of any more, he thought, and he felt so old and hopeless and dumb, that he almost didn't care by then which son it was if he'd only stop badgering him.

He sent out for a drink and a sandwich, which revived him a little, and then with a sudden rush of emotion, his all but useless eyes welling with tears, he reached out and pulled the young man to him and kissed him. Clover and timothy, black earth, horse manure, rain—his ears and his eyes were all shot, he thought, and he couldn't even tell what he was touching half the time what with his bad circulation, but at least he still had a nose that worked, and by now the lump in his throat was so big he could hardly get the words out of his mouth.

"See, the smell of my son is as the smell of a field which the Lord has blessed," he said (Genesis 27:27), and then not caring whether it was Esau or Jacob or Napoleon Bonaparte who was there on his knees before him, he gave out with a blessing that made all the other blessings he'd ever given sound like a tin whistle.

Jacob had to get out of town in a hurry when Esau found out, and he was gone off and on for twenty years, but he came back again finally just in time to see Isaac once more before he died although it's doubtful that Isaac was in any condition by then to know much about it. Then Jacob and Esau together, the guller and the gulled, buried him as by then they had also buried the hatchet, and thus the shadowy old man disappeared permanently into the shadows at last.

(Genesis 18:1–15, 21–22:19, 25:7–11, 35:27–29)

ISAIAH

There were banks of candles flickering in the distance and clouds of incense thickening the air with holiness and stinging his eyes, and high above him, as if it had always been there but was only now seen for what it was (like a face in the leaves of a tree or a bear among the stars), there was the Mystery Itself whose gown was the incense and the candles a dusting of gold at the hem. There were winged creatures shouting back and forth the way excited children shout to each other when dusk calls them home, and the whole vast, reeking place started to shake beneath his feet like a wagon going over cobbles, and he cried out, "O God, I am done for! I am foul of mouth and the member of a foul-mouthed race. With my own two eyes I have seen him. I'm a goner and sunk." Then one of the winged things touched his mouth with fire and said, "There, it will be all right now," and the Mystery Itself said, "Who will it be?" and with charred lips he said, "Me," and Mystery said "GO."

Mystery said, "Go give the deaf Hell till you're blue in the face and go show the blind Heaven till you drop in your tracks because they'd sooner eat ground glass than swallow the bitter pill that puts roses in the cheeks and a gleam in the eye. Go do it."

Isaiah said, "Do it till when?"

Mystery said, "Till Hell freezes over."

Mystery said, "Do it till the cows come home."

And that is what a prophet does for a living and, starting from the year that King Uzziah died when he saw and heard all these things, Isaiah went and did it.

(Isaiah 6)

Jj

JACOB (See also DINAH, ESAU, ISAAC, RACHEL, REBECCA)

The Book of Genesis makes no attempt to conceal the fact that Jacob was, among other things, a crook. What's more, you get the feeling that whoever wrote up his seamy adventures got a real kick out of them.

Twice he cheated his lame-brained brother Esau out of what was coming to him (*see* ESAU). At least once he took advantage of his old father, Isaac's, blindness and played him for a sucker (*see* ISAAC). He out-did his double-crossing father-in-law, Laban, by conning him out of most of his livestock, and later on, when Laban was looking the other way, by sneaking off with not only both the man's daughters but just about everything else that wasn't nailed down including his household gods. Jacob was never satisfied. He wanted the moon, and if he'd ever managed to bilk Heaven out of that, he would have been back the next morning for the stars to go with it. But then one day he learned a marvelous lesson in a marvelous and unexpected way.

It happened just after he'd ripped Esau off for the second time and was making his getaway into the hill country to the north. When sunset came and nobody seemed to be after him, he decided that it was safe to camp out for the night, and having left in too much of a hurry to take his bedroll with him, tucked a stone under his head for a pillow and prepared to go to sleep. You might think that what happened next was that he lay there all night bug-eyed as a result of his guilty conscience or if he did finally manage to drop off, that he was tormented by conscience-stricken dreams, but neither of these was the case. Instead he dropped off like a baby in a cradle and dreamed the kind of dreams you would have thought were reserved for the high saints.

He dreamed that there was a ladder reaching up to heaven and that there were angels moving up and down it with golden sandals and rainbow-colored wings and that standing somewhere above it was God himself. And the words God spoke in the dream were not the chewing-out you might have expected but something altogether different. God told him that the land he was lying on was to belong to him and his descendants and that someday his descendants would become a great nation and a great blessing to all the other nations on earth. And as if that wasn't enough, he then added a personal P.S. by saying, "Behold, I am with you and will keep you wherever you go."

It wasn't Holy Hell that God gave him, in other words, but Holy Heaven, not to mention the marvelous lesson thrown in for good measure. The lesson was, needless to say, that even for a dyed-in-the-wool, double-barreled con artist like

Jacob there are a few things in this world you can't get but can only be given, and one of these things is love in general, and another is the love of God in particular.

Jacob didn't have to climb his ladder to bilk Heaven of the moon and the stars, even if that had been possible, because the moon and the stars looked like jelly-beans compared to what God and the angels were using the ladder to hand down to him for free.

Another part of the lesson was that, luckily for Jacob, God doesn't love people because of who they are but because of who he is. *It's on the house* is one way of saying it and *it's by grace* is another, just as it was by grace that it was Jacob of all people who became not only the father of the twelve tribes of Israel but the many times great grandfather of Jesus of Nazareth, and just as it was by grace that Jesus of Nazareth was born into this world at all.

(Genesis 25:24–28:17)

JAEL

A Canaanite war-lord named Sisera had recently been trounced by an Israelite strong-man named Barak and was heading for the border to save his skin. On the way, he was invited to hide out with a Kenite woman named Jael, who belonged to a tribe which had not been involved in the skirmish at all. This was his second bad break that day.

Jael was all smiles as she issued her invitation and gave him the red carpet treatment. She fixed him a drink and suggested he stretch out for a while on the couch. While he was asleep, she crept in and disposed of him by the ingenious if cumbersome technique of hammering a tent-peg in one temple and out the other.

The female judge Deborah (q.v.) wrote a song in her honor in which she referred to her as "most blessed among women" for the job she had done, and Jael has been remembered as a great hero and patriot ever since.

In view of the fact that her victim (a) was her guest and (b) was asleep and (c) had never harmed a hair of either her head or her people's, it would seem that to call her deed heroic is to stretch the term to the breaking point. As for calling it patriotic, if she had done it for love of country—maybe. But (a) her country had no quarrel with Sisera and (b) if she killed him for anything but kicks, it was out of love for nothing more exalted than the idea of maybe getting a pay-off from the Israelites the next time they hit town. It is not the only instance, of course, of how people in wartime get medals for doing what in peacetime would get them the chair.

(Judges 4–5)

JEREMIAH

The word *jeremiad* means a doleful and thunderous denunciation, and its derivation is no mystery. There was nothing in need of denunciation that Jeremiah didn't denounce. He denounced the king and the clergy. He denounced recreational sex and extramarital jamborees. He denounced the rich for exploiting the poor, and he denounced the poor for deserving no better. He denounced the way every new god that came sniffing around had them all after him like so many bitches in heat; and right at the very gates of the Temple he told them that if they thought God was impressed by all the mumbo-jumbo that went on in there, they ought to have their heads examined.

When some of them took to indulging in a little human sacrifice on the side, he appeared with a clay pot which he smashed into smithereens to show them what God planned to do to them as soon as he got around to it. He even denounced God himself for saddling him with the job of trying to reform such a pack of hyenas, degenerates, ninnies. "You have deceived me," he said, shaking his fist. You are "like a deceitful brook, like waters that fail" (Jeremiah 15:18), and God took it.

But the people didn't. When he told them that the Babylonians were going to come in and rip them to shreds as they richly deserved, they worked him over and threw him in jail. When the Babylonians did come in and not only ripped them to shreds but tore down their precious Temple and ran off with all the expensive hardware, he told them that since it was God's judgment upon them, they better submit to it or else; whereupon they threw him into an open cistern that happened to be handy. Luckily the cistern had no water in it, but Jeremiah sank into the muck up to his armpits and stayed there till an Ethiopian eunuch pulled him out with a rope.

He told them that if they were so crazy about circumcision, then they ought to get their minds above their navels for once and try circumcising "the foreskins of their hearts" (Jeremiah 4:4); and the only hope he saw for them was that someday God would put the law in their hearts too instead of in the books, but that was a long way off.

At his lowest ebb he cursed the day he was born like Job, and you can hardly blame him. He had spent his life telling them to shape up with the result that they were in just about as miserable shape as they'd have been if he'd never bothered, and urging them to submit to Babylon as the judgment of God when all their patriotic instincts made that sound like the worst kind of defeatism and treachery.

He also told them that, Babylonian occupation or no Babylonian occupation, they should stick around so that someday they could rise up and be a new nation again; and then the first chance they got, a bunch of them beat it over the border into Egypt. What's even worse, they dragged old Jeremiah, kicking and screaming, along with them, which seems the final irony: that he, who had fought so long and hard against all forms of idolatry—the Nation as idol, the Temple as idol, the King as idol—should at last have been tucked into their baggage like a kind of rabbit's foot or charm against the evil eye or idol himself.

What became of him in Egypt afterwards is not known, but the tradition is that his own people finally got so exasperated with him there that they stoned him to death. If that is true, nothing could be less surprising.

(The Book of Jeremiah)

JESUS (*See also* BARABBAS, CAESAR AUGUSTUS,
CAIAPHAS, DAVID, ETHIOPIAN EUNUCH, GABRIEL, HEROD
THE GREAT, HEROD ANTIPAS, JACOB, JOHN THE
BAPTIST, JOHN THE EVANGELIST, JOSEPH OF ARIMATHEA,
JOSEPH THE HUSBAND OF MARY, JUDAS, LAZARUS,
LUKE, MARK, MARY, MARY MAGDALENE, NATHANIEL,
NICODEMUS, PAUL, PETER, PILATE, QUIRINIUS, RAHAB,
SIMEON, THOMAS, WISE MEN, YAHWEH, ZACCHEUS)

Maybe any one day of a life, even the most humdrum, has
in it something of the mystery of that life as a whole.

People had been flocking up to Jesus the way they always
seemed to when word got around that he was in the neighborhood. A Roman officer came up to ask if he would do
something for a paralyzed servant back home, and Jesus said
he'd go have a look at him. When the officer said he hated to
take that much of his time and asked if he couldn't just do
something from right there where they were standing, Jesus
was so impressed by the way the man trusted him that he
told him he'd see to it that what he trusted would happen
would happen indeed, and when the officer got home, he

found his servant up and around again. Later on, when Jesus dropped in at Peter's house, he found Peter's mother-in-law in bed with a fever, and all he did that time was touch the old lady's hand, but that turned out to be all it took.

A scribe showed up and in a burst of enthusiasm said he was all set to follow him any place he went, to which Jesus answered, "Foxes have holes, and birds have nests, but if you stick with me, you'll find yourself out in the cold" (Matthew 8:20). One of the disciples asked for a few days off to attend his father's funeral, and Jesus said, "Look, you've got to follow me. When life's at stake, burying the dead is for dead-heads" (Matthew 8:22). When he saw a big crowd approaching, he figured he didn't have enough steam left to do much for them that day, so he went and climbed into a boat for a few hours' peace only to find that the disciples were hot on his heels and wanted to go along too. So he took them. Then he lay down in the stern of the boat with a pillow under his head, Mark says (Mark 4:34), and went to sleep.

Matthew leaves out the details about the stern and the pillow (see MATTHEW) presumably because he thought they weren't important, which of course they're not, and yet the account would be greatly impoverished without them. There's so little about him in the Gospels you can actually see.

He didn't doze off in the bow where the spray would get him and the whitecaps slapped harder. He climbed back into the stern instead. There was a pillow under his head. Maybe somebody put it there for him. Maybe they didn't think to put it there till after he'd gone to sleep, and then somebody lifted his head a little off the hard deck and slipped it under.

He must have gone out like a light because Mark says the storm didn't wake him, not even when the waves got so high they started washing in over the sides. They let him sleep on until finally they were so scared they couldn't stand it any longer and woke him up. They addressed him respectfully enough as Teacher, but what they said was reproachful, petulant almost. "Don't you see that we're all *drowning?*" (Mark 4:38).

It was the wind rather than the disciples that Jesus seems to have spoken to first, as soon as he'd gotten his eyes open. "He rebuked it," Mark says (Mark 4:38). CUT THAT OUT!—you can almost picture him staring it down with the hair lashing his face as he holds on to the gunnels to keep from being blown overboard. He was gentler with the sea. "Take it easy," he said. "Quiet down." When it came the disciples' turn, he said, "Why did you panic?" and then "What kind of faith do you call that?" but they were so impressed to find that the wind had stopped blowing and the sea had flattened out again that they didn't get around to answering him (Mark 4:39–41).

On the far shore there was a cemetery where a crazy man lived covered with scars from where he was always smashing at himself with stones and from the chains they tried to tie him down with when he got even more violent than usual. As soon as the boat landed, he came gibbering out from behind the graves and went tearing down to the beach, but as soon as he saw Jesus, he stopped in his tracks and quieted down. They talked together a little, and then Jesus healed him.

The Roman officer, the sick old lady, the overenthusiastic scribe, the terrified disciples, the lunatic—something of who he was and what he was like and what it was like to be with him filters through each meeting as it comes along, but for some reason it's the moment in the boat that says most. The way he lay down, bone tired, and fell asleep with the sound of the lapping waves in his ears. The way, when they woke him, he opened his eyes to the howling storm and to all the other howling things that he must have known were in the cards for him and that his nap had been a few moments of vacation from. The helplessness of the disciples and the way he spoke to them. The things he said to the wind and to the sea.

Lamb of God, Rose of Sharon, Prince of Peace—none of the things people have found to call him has ever managed to say it quite right. You can see why when he told people to follow him, they often did, even if they backed out later when they started to catch on to what lay ahead. If you're religiously inclined, you can see why they went even so far as to call him Messiah, the Lord's Anointed, the Son of God, and call him these things still, some of them. And even if you're not religiously inclined, you can see why it is you might give your immortal soul, if you thought you had one to give, to have been the one to raise that head a little from the hard deck and slip a pillow under it.

(Matthew 8:5–34, compare Mark 4:35–41)

JEZEBEL (*See* AHAB, ELIJAH)

JOB

Job was the richest man around, but in a single day he was wiped out. The Sabeans ran off with his asses and oxen and slaughtered the hired hands. Lightning struck his sheep barn and burned up the whole flock, not to mention the shepherds. The Chaldeans rustled his camels and made short work of the camel drivers. And a hurricane hit with such devastating effect the house where his seven sons and three daughters were having a party that there wasn't enough of them left in the wreckage to identify.

What happened next was that Job came down with leprosy. And what happened after that was that he cursed the day that he was born. He said that if he had his way, it would be stricken off the calendar entirely and never so much as mentioned again. He prayed to die, but his heart went on beating. He prayed for the sun to go out like a match, but it kept on shining. His wife advised him to curse God and then go hang himself, but he stopped just short of that because he was a very good man and a very religious man and there were some lengths to which, even though he was almost out of his head with the horror of it all, he couldn't quite bring himself to go. And that was the crux of his problem—the fact that he was a very good and a very religious man and knew it. Why had God let such things happen to him?

He had four well-meaning but insufferable friends who came over to cheer him up and try to explain it. They said that anybody with enough sense to come in out of the rain knew that God was just. They said that anybody old enough to spell his own name knew that since God was just, he made bad things happen to bad people and good things happen to good people. They said that such being the case, you didn't need a Harvard diploma to figure out that since bad things had happened to Job, then *ipso facto* he must have done something bad himself. But Job hadn't, and he said so, and that's not all he said either. "Worthless physicians are you all," he said. "Oh that you would keep silent, and it would be your wisdom" (Job 13:4–5). They were a bunch of theological quacks, in other words, and the smartest thing they could do was shut up. But they were too busy explaining things to listen.

Eliphaz the Temanite proceeded to make a few helpful suggestions about some of the bad things that Job must have done and then let slip his mind. He must have robbed a few beggars of the rags on their backs, he said. He must have refused food to some poor soul who was starving to death. There must have been several widows and orphans he'd ground his heel in the faces of without stopping to think what he was doing. But Job didn't even dignify these charges by refuting them. He talked about God instead.

There had been a time when God and he had been *like that,* he said, holding up side by side what the leprosy had left of two fingers. There was a time "when his lamp shone upon my head," he said, "and by his light I walked through darkness. When the Almighty was with me, and when my children were about me" (Job 29:3, 5), and then he had to stop for a few minutes and blow what was left of his nose before going on.

The question, he said once he'd had time to pull himself back together, was where was God now? He had looked for him in front, and he had looked for him in back; he had looked for him to the right, and he had looked for him to the left; but he wasn't anywhere to be found. If he only knew where God might be keeping himself, he'd go tell him his troubles and get an explanation at least, but God had made himself scarce as hen's teeth, and looking for him was like looking for a needle in a haystack.

"God has cast me into the mire, and I have become like dust and ashes," he said, too miserable to worry about mixing his metaphors. "I cry to thee, and thou dost not answer me," he said, "and with the might of thy hand thou dost persecute me" (Job 30:19–21). It was the closest he had come yet to taking his wife's advice and calling him a sonofabitch. "My skin turns black and falls from me," he said (Job 30:30) and then took advantage of a long speech by a friend named Elihu to change a few of his dressings.

Elihu went over many of the same points his colleagues had already ticked off and then added the idea that the destruction of all Job's property and the death of all his children and his leprosy were probably just God's way of helping him to improve his character and sharpen his sensitivities. "He delivers the afflicted by their afflictions," he explained, "and opens their ears by adversity" (Job 36:15), but Job had no chance to respond to this new and comforting insight because at that point another speaker made himself heard, and this time the speaker was God.

Just the way God cleared his throat almost blasted Job off his feet, and that was only for starters. It is the most gorgeous speech that God makes in the whole Old Testament, and it is composed almost entirely of the most gorgeous and preposterous questions that have ever been asked by God or anybody else.

"Have you entered into the springs of the sea, or walked in the recesses of the deep?" he asked. "Where is the dwelling of light? Have you entered the storehouses of the snow, or has the rain a father? Can you bind the chain of the Pleiades? Who has put wisdom in the clouds or given understanding to the mists?" (Job 38 passim). And by this time he was just starting to get wound up.

"Is the wild ox willing to serve you?" he asked. "Will he spend the night at your crib? The wings of the ostrich wave proudly, but are they the pinions and plumage of love? Have you given the horse strength? Have you clothed his neck with thunder, who says among the trumpets Ha, ha! and smells the battle afar off? Does the hawk fly by your wisdom and stretch her wings toward the south?" (Job 39 passim).

There was obviously only one thing for Job to say, and he said it. "Behold, I am of small account. What shall I answer thee?" he said, coming out with that one frail question of his own. "I will proceed no further" (Job 40:3–5). But God wasn't through yet.

You can think of God as a great cosmic bully here if you want, but you can think of him also as a great cosmic artist, a singer, say, of such power and magnificence and so caught up in the incandescence of his own art that he never notices that he has long since ruptured the eardrums of his listeners and reduced them to quivering pulp. "Have you an arm like

God, and can you thunder with a voice like his?" he asked (Job 40:9), and then he launched off into a devastating aria about Behemoth, the hippopotamus he had made, and Leviathan, the crocodile he had made, challenging Job, or anybody else if they thought they could, to take them for walks on leashes or pierce their armored hides with cold steel.

You feel that God had only paused to catch his breath when Job saw his chance to break in again at last. "I have uttered what I did not understand, things too wonderful for me, which I did not know," he said (Job 42:3). And then he said something else.

All his life he had heard about God, about his glory and his holiness, about his terrible wrath and his great mercy, about the way he had created the earth and all its creatures and set the sun, moon, and stars in the sky so there would always be light to see by and beauty to gladden the heart. He had sometimes thrilled and sometimes trembled at the sound of these descriptions, and they had made such an impression on him over the years that not even the terrible things that had happened to him or the terrible question as to *why* they had happened or the miserable answers to that question which his friends had proposed could quite make him curse God as had been suggested although there were a few times when he came uncomfortably close to it. But now it was no longer a matter of hearing descriptions of God because finally he had heard and seen him for himself.

He had seen the great glory so shot through with sheer, fierce light and life and gladness, had heard the great voice raised in song so full of terror and wildness and beauty, that from that moment on, nothing else mattered. All possible questions melted like mist, and all possible explanations withered like grass, and all the bad times of his life together with all the good times were so caught up into the fathomless life of this God, who had bent down to speak with him though by comparison he was no more than a fleck of dust on the head of a pin in the lapel of a dancing flea, that all he could say was, "I had heard of thee by the hearing of the ear, but now my eye sees thee; therefore I despise myself and repent in dust and ashes" (Job 42:5–6).

But God didn't let him despise himself for long. He turned to the garrulous friends and said, "You have not spoken of me what is right as my servant Job has" (Job 42:7), with the clear implication that Job had been right in standing up to him if only because it showed he was worth listening to as his friends preeminently were not. And then he gave back to Job more riches than he had ever had before together with his health, and Job lived to have a whole new set of children and to see them through four generations before he died old and full of days.

As for the children he had lost when the house blew down, not to mention all his employees, he never got an explanation about them because he never asked for one, and the reason he never asked for one was that he knew that even if God gave him one that made splendid sense out of all the pain and suffering that had ever been since the world began, it was no longer splendid sense that he needed because with his own eyes he had beheld, and not as a stranger, the one who in the end clothed all things, no matter how small or confused or in pain, with his own splendor.

And that was more than sufficient.

(The Book of Job)

JOHN THE BAPTIST (*See also* SALOME)

John the Baptist didn't fool around. He lived in the wilderness around the Dead Sea. He subsisted on a starvation diet, and so did his disciples. He wore clothes that even the rummage sale people wouldn't have handled. When he preached, it was fire and brimstone every time.

The Kingdom was coming all right, he said, but if you thought it was going to be a pink tea, you'd better think again. If you didn't shape up, God would give you the axe

like an elm with the blight or toss you into the incinerator like what's left over when you've lambasted the good out of the wheat. He said being a Jew wouldn't get you any more points than being a Hottentot, and one of his favorite ways of addressing his congregation was as a snake pit. Your only hope, he said, was to clean up your life as if your life depended on it, which it did, and get baptized in a hurry as a sign that you had. Some people thought he was Elijah come back from the grave, and some others thought he was the Messiah, but John would have none of either. "I'm the one yelling himself blue in the face in the wilderness," he said, quoting Isaiah. "I'm the one trying to knock some sense into your heads" (Matthew 3:3).

One day who should show up but Jesus. John knew who he was in a second. "You're the one who should be baptizing me," he said (Matthew 3:14), but Jesus insisted, and so they waded out into the Jordan together, and it was John who did the honors.

John apparently had second thoughts about him later on, however, and it's no great wonder. Where John preached grim justice and pictured God as a steely-eyed thresher of grain, Jesus preached forgiving love and pictured God as the host at a marvelous party or a father who can't bring himself to throw his children out even when they spit in his eye. Where John said people had better save their skins before it was too late, Jesus said it was God who saved their skins, and even if you blew your whole bankroll on liquor and sex like the Prodigal Son, it still wasn't too late. Where John ate locusts and honey in the wilderness with the church crowd, Jesus ate what he felt like in Jerusalem with as sleazy a bunch as you could expect to find. Where John crossed to the other side of the street if he saw any sinners heading his way, Jesus seems to have preferred their company to the W.C.T.U., the Stewardship Committee, and the World Council of Churches rolled into one. Where John baptized, Jesus healed.

Finally John decided to settle the thing once and for all and sent a couple of his disciples to put it to Jesus straight. "John wants to know if you're the One we've been waiting for or whether we should cool our heels a while longer," they said (Luke 7:20), and Jesus said, "You go tell John what you've seen around here. Tell him there are people who have sold their seeing-eye dogs and taken up bird-watching. Tell him there are people who've traded in aluminum walkers for hiking boots. Tell him the down-and-out have turned into the up-and-coming and a lot of deadbeats are living it up for the first time in their lives. And three cheers for the one who can swallow all this without gagging" (Luke 7:22–23). When they asked Jesus what he thought about John, he said, "They don't come any better, but when the Big Party Up There really gets off the ground even John will look like about two cents by comparison" (Luke 7:28).

Nobody knows how John reacted when his disciples came back with Jesus' message, but maybe he remembered how he had felt that day when he'd first seen him heading toward him through the tall grass along the river-bank and how his heart had skipped a beat when he heard himself say, "Behold the Lamb of God who taketh away the sins of the world" (John 1:29), and maybe after he remembered all that and put it together with what they'd told him about the deadbeats and the aluminum walkers, he decided he must have been right the first time.

(Luke 3:1–22, 7:18–35, Matthew 3:1–17, 9:14–17,

John 1:1–34)

JOHN THE EVANGELIST

John was a poet, and he knew about words. He knew that all men and all women are mysteries known only to themselves until they speak a word that opens up the mystery. He knew that the words people speak have their life in them just as surely as they have their breath in them. He knew that the words people speak have dynamite in them and that a word may be all it takes to set somebody's heart on fire or break it in two. He knew that words break silence and that the word that is spoken is the word that is heard and may even be answered. And at the beginning of his gospel he wrote a poem about the Word that God spoke.

When God speaks, things happen because the words of God aren't just as good as his deeds, they are his deeds. When God speaks his word, John says, creation happens, and when God speaks to his creation, what comes out is not ancient Hebrew or the King James Version or a sentiment suitable for framing in the pastor's study. On the contrary. "The word became flesh," John says (1:14), and that means that when God wanted to say what God is all about and what man is all about and what life is all about, it wasn't a sound that emerged but a man. Jesus was his name. He was dynamite. He was the word of God.

As this might lead you to expect, the Gospel of John is as different from the other three as night from day. Matthew quotes Scripture, Mark lists miracles, Luke reels off parables, and each has his own special axe to grind too, but the one thing they all did in common was to say something also about the thirty-odd years Jesus lived on this earth, the kinds of things he did and said and what he got for his pains as well as what the world got for his pains too. John, on the other hand, clearly has something else in mind, and if you didn't happen to know, you'd hardly guess that his Jesus and the Jesus of the other three gospels are the same man.

John says nothing about when or where or how he was born. He says nothing about how the baptist baptized him. There's no account of the temptation in John, or the transfiguration, nothing about how he told people to eat bread and drink wine in his memory once in a while, or how he sweated blood in the garden the night they arrested him, or how he was tried before the Sanhedrin as well as before Pilate. There's nothing in John about the terrible moment when he cried out that God had forsaken him at the very time he needed him most. Jesus doesn't tell even a single parable in John. So what then, according to John, does Jesus do?

He speaks words. He speaks poems that sound much like John's poems, and the poems are about himself. Even when he works his miracles, you feel he's thinking less about the human needs of the people he's working them for than about something else he's got to say about who he is and what he's there to get done. When he feeds a big, hungry crowd on hardly enough to fill a grocery bag, for instance, he says, "I am the bread of life. He who comes to me shall not hunger, and he who believes in me shall never thirst" (6:35). When he raises his old friend Lazarus from the dead, he says, "I am the resurrection and the life. He who believes in me, though he die, yet shall he live, and whoever lives and believes in me shall never die" (11:25–26). "I am the door," he says, "and if any one enters by me, he will be saved" (10:9). "I am the good shepherd" (10:14), "the light of the world" (8:12), "I am the way, the truth, and the life," he says (14:6) and "I and the Father are one" (10:30).

You miss the Jesus of Matthew, Mark, and Luke of course—the one who got mad and tired and took naps in boats. You miss the Jesus who healed people because he felt sorry for them and made jokes about camels squeezing through the eyes of needles and had a soft spot in his heart for easy-going ladies and children who didn't worry about Heaven like the disciples because in a way they were already there. There's nothing he doesn't know in John, nothing he can't do, and when they take him in the end, you feel he could blow them right off the map if he felt like it. Majestic, mystical, aloof almost, the Jesus of the Fourth Gospel walks three feet off the ground, you feel, and you can't help wishing that once in a while he'd come down to earth.

But that's just the point, of course—John's point. It's not the Jesus people knew on earth that he's mainly talking about, and everybody agrees that the story about how he saved the adulteress's skin by saying, "Let him who is without sin cast the first stone" (8:7) must have been added by somebody else, it seems so out of place with all the rest.

Jesus, for John, is the Jesus he knew in his own heart and the one he believed everybody else could know too if they only kept their hearts open. He is Jesus as the Word that breaks the heart and sets the feet to dancing and stirs tigers in the blood. He is the Jesus John loved not just because he'd healed the sick and fed the hungry but because he'd saved the world. Jesus as the *mot juste* of God.

JONAH (*See also* WHALE)

Within a few minutes of swallowing the prophet Jonah, the whale suffered a severe attack of acid indigestion, and it's not hard to see why. Jonah had a disposition that was enough to curdle milk.

When God ordered him to go to Nineveh and tell them there to shape up and get saved, the expression on Jonah's face was that of a man who has just gotten a whiff of trouble in his septic tank. In the first place, the Ninevites were foreigners and thus off his beat. In the second place, far from wanting to see them get saved, nothing would have pleased him more than to see them get what he thought they had coming to them.

It was as the result of a desperate attempt to get himself out of the assignment that he got himself swallowed by the whale instead; but the whale couldn't stomach him for long, and in the end Jonah went ahead, and with a little more prodding from God, did what he'd been told. He hated every minute of it, however, and when the Ninevites succumbed to his eloquence and promised to shape up, he sat down under a leafy castor oil plant to shade him from the blistering sun and smouldered inwardly. It was an opening that God could not resist.

He caused the castor oil plant to shrivel up to the last leaf, and when Jonah got all upset at being back in the ghastly heat again, God pretended to misunderstand what was bugging him.

"Here you are, all upset out of pity for one small castor oil plant that has shriveled up," he said, "so what's wrong with having pity for this whole place that's headed for Hell in a handcart if something's not done about it?" (Jonah 4:10–11).

It is one of the rare instances in the Old Testament of God's wry sense of humor, and it seems almost certain that Jonah didn't fail to appreciate it.

(The Book of Jonah)

JONATHAN (See also MEPHIBOSHETH)

When King Saul found his oldest son, Jonathan, siding with David, whom he considered his arch-enemy, he cursed him out by saying that he had made David a friend "to your own shame, and to the shame of your mother's nakedness" (1 Samuel 20:30). They are strong words, and some have interpreted them as meaning that Saul suspected a sexual relationship between the two young men.

This view can be further buttressed by such verses as "The soul of Jonathan was knit to the soul of David, and Jonathan loved him as his own soul" (1 Samuel 18:1) and the words David spoke when he learned of Jonathan's death, "Your love

to me was wonderful, passing the love of women" (2 Samuel 1:26). When David and Jonathan said goodbye to each other for almost the last time, they "kissed one another and wept" (1 Samuel 20:41), we're told, and there are undoubtedly those who would point to that too as evidence.

There seem to be at least three things to say in response to all this.

The first is that both emotions and the language used to express them ran a good deal higher in the ancient Near East than they do in Little Rock, Arkansas, or Boston, Massachusetts, or even Los Angeles, California, and for that and other reasons the theory that such passages as have been cited necessarily indicate a homosexual relationship is almost certainly false.

The second is that it's sad, putting it rather mildly, that we live at a time when in many quarters two men can't embrace or weep together or speak of loving one another without arousing the suspicion that they must also go to bed together.

Third, in the unlikely event that there was a sexual dimension to the friendship between Jonathan and David, it is significant that the only one to see it as shameful was King Saul, who was a manic depressive with homicidal tendencies and an eventual suicide.

Everywhere else in the Book of Samuel it seems to be assumed that what was important about the relationship was not what may or may not have been its physical side but the affection, respect, and faithfulness that kept it alive through thick and thin until finally Jonathan was killed in battle and David rent his garments and wept over him.

(1 Samuel 19–2 Samuel 1, passim)

JOSEPH AND HIS BRETHREN

Joseph's brothers tried to murder him by throwing him into a pit, but if they had ever been brought to trial, they wouldn't have needed Clarence Darrow to get them an acquittal in any court in the land. Not only did Joseph have offensive dreams in which he was Mr. Big and they were all groveling at his feet but he recounted them in sickening detail at the breakfast table the next morning. He was also his father's pet, and they seethed at the sight of the many-colored coat he flaunted while they were running around in T-shirts and dirty jeans.

After tossing him into the pit, the brothers decided to tell Jacob, their father, that his fair-haired boy had had a fatal tangle with bob-cats, and in order to convince him, they produced a shirt that they'd dipped in goat's blood. Jacob was convinced, and they didn't even have to worry too much about the lie they'd told him because by the time they got around to telling it, they figured that one way or another it, or something like it, must have come true.

Unknown to them, however, Joseph was rescued from the pit by some traveling salesmen who happened to be passing by and eventually wound up as a slave in Egypt where he was bought by an Army man named Potiphar. He got into trouble over an embarrassing misunderstanding with Potiphar's prehensile wife and did some time in jail for it as a result, but Pharaoh got wind of the fact that he was big on dream interpretations and had him sprung to see what he could do with a couple of wild ones he'd had himself. When Joseph passed with flying colors, Pharaoh promoted him to be head of the Department of Agriculture and eventually his right-hand man.

Years later, Joseph's brothers, who had long since succeeded in putting him out of their minds, turned up in Egypt too, looking for something to eat because they were having a famine back home. Joseph knew who they were right off the bat, but because he was wearing his fancy uniform and speaking Egyptian, they didn't recognize him.

Joseph couldn't resist getting a little of his own back for a while. He pretended he thought they were spies. He gave them some grain to take home but made one of them stay behind as a hostage. He planted some silverware in their luggage and accused them of copping it. But though with part of himself he was presumably getting a kick out of all this, with another part he was so moved and pleased to be back in touch with his own flesh and blood after so long that every once in a while he had to get out of the room in a hurry so they wouldn't see how choked up he was and discover his true identity.

Finally he'd had enough. He told them who he was, and they all fell into each other's arms and wept. He then invited them to come live with him in Egypt and to bring old Jacob along with them too who was so delighted to find Joseph alive after all these years that he didn't even seem too upset about the trick that had been played on him with the bloody shirt.

The real moment of truth came, however, when Jacob finally died. Generous and forgiving as Joseph had been, his brothers couldn't avoid the nasty suspicion that once the old man wasn't around any more to put in a good word for them, Joseph might start thinking again about what it had felt like when they tossed him into that pit and decide to pay them back as they deserved. So they went to see him, fell down on their knees, and begged his pardon.

Joseph's answer rings out like a bell. "Don't be scared. Of course you're pardoned," he said. "Do you think I'm God to grovel before me like that?" In the old days, of course, God was just who he'd rather suspected he was and the dreams where they groveled were his all-time favorites.

Almost as much as it is the story of how Israel was saved from famine and extinction, it is the story of how Joseph was saved as a human being. It would be interesting to know which of the two achievements cost God the greater effort and which was the one he was prouder of.

(Genesis 37–50)

JOSEPH OF ARIMATHEA

As a prominent member of the Jewish establishment, Joseph of Arimathea needed guts to go to Pilate and ask for the dead body of Jesus so he could give it a decent burial. It is presumably no easier for a closet Christian to come out of the closet than it is for anybody else, and you can't help ad-

miring him for it. In view of the events of Easter morning, however, you can't help noting that if he'd only waited a few days, he could have spared himself a thumping bill from the undertaker.

It is important to give Joseph of Arimathea his due for his mortuary solicitude, but at the same time it is hard not to see him as the first of many Christians who spend so much time stewing about the blood of the lamb that they lose sight of the fact that the lamb has long since gone on to greener pastures where he's kicking up his heels in the sunshine and calling to others to come join the dance.

(Luke 23:50–56)

JOSEPH THE HUSBAND OF MARY

You can hardly blame Joseph for considering divorce when he discovered that, through no fault of his, Mary was pregnant. Nevertheless, when it was explained to him, he took it like a man, and all was forgiven. As soon as he got word in a dream that King Herod was planning to massacre all male babies in the neighborhood in hopes that the newborn Messiah would be one of them, he took the child and Mary and beat it to Egypt where he had the good sense to remain till he found Herod's name in the obituary column.

Later on, when they lost Jesus in Jerusalem at the age of twelve, Joseph was as nervous a wreck over it as Mary and every bit as delighted once the boy was found.

When Matthew in his gospel records Jesus's genealogy, he traces it back through his mother's line in deference to the doctrine that the one whose son Jesus was was God. When Luke records it, on the other hand, although he was no less a true believer, he makes no bones about listing Joseph as the father of Jesus and tracing the line back through him.

Since Jesus himself never seems to have worried much about theology, it is hard not to believe that, for auld lang syne, he would have preferred Luke's version.

(Matthew 1–2, Luke 2:41–51, 3:23–38)

JOSHUA (*See also* RAHAB)

Moses was a hard act to follow. After the tired old man breathed his last on the slopes of Mt. Pisgah overlooking the Promised Land, which he never quite made it to, the job of leading the Israelites on in fell to Joshua. Since the Promised Land was inhabited by a group of native Canaanite tribes who weren't about to give it up without an argument, the result was years of war at its cruelest and most savage. And in the eyes of Joshua and his people, it wasn't just any old war. It was a holy war. It was Yahweh they were fighting for because the land they were out to get, come Hell or high water, was the land that centuries before, in Abraham's time, Yahweh had promised them so they could settle down in it and become a great nation and a blessing to all nations. Prisoners weren't supposed to be taken, and spoils weren't supposed to be divided, because Yahweh was the one they all belonged to. Ai, Jericho, Gibeon—cities fell like clay pigeons at Joshua's feet, and everything that would burn was put to the torch, and everything that wouldn't, like men, women and children, was put to the sword. Holy wars are the unholiest kind.

The battle at Gibeon was one of the worst parts of it. Five Amorite kings were drawn up against the Israelites, and Joshua launched his attack just before dawn. His men leapt out of the mists with a terrible light in their eyes. There was a wild storm with hailstones as big as hand-grenades. The Amorites panicked. The slaughter was on. It was a long, bloody massacre, and in order to have enough daylight to finish it by, Joshua fixed the sun with his stern military gaze and gave it his orders.

"Sun, stand thou still at Gibeon!" he said (Joshua 10:12), and because he was in command of the operation and because Yahweh was in command of him, the sun snapped to attention and kept shining till the job was done. It was the longest day on record, and when it was finally over, the ground was strewn with the dead, and the mutilated bodies of the five kings were hanging from five trees like meat at a butcher shop.

With one exception, there was nothing that Joshua hadn't been able to see in the prolonged and relentless light the sun had supplied him with. The one exception was that the God he was fighting for was the God of the Amorites too whether they realized it or not. But Yahweh saw it and brooded over it and more than a thousand years later, through the mouth of his Anointed, spoke about it.

"Blessed are those who mourn, for they shall be comforted," he said (Matthew 5:4), and then he also blessed the peacemakers so that even without any extra sunshine everybody would be able to see that peace is better than even the holiest wars, especially the kind of peace which not even a holy terror like Joshua can either give or take away.

(Joshua 10)

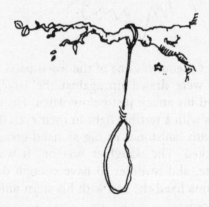

JUDAS

Nobody can be sure, of course, why Judas sold Jesus out although according to John's gospel, he already had a reputation for dipping into the poor box from time to time so the cash may have been part of it. If, like the other disciples, he was perennially worried about where he stood in the pecking order, he may also have been reacting to some imagined slight. Maybe he thought his job as treasurer to the outfit was beneath him. Another possibility is that he had gotten fed up with waiting for Jesus to take the world by storm and hoped that betraying him might force him to show his hand at last. Or maybe, because nothing human is ever uncomplicated, something of all of these was involved. Anyway, whatever his reasons were, the whole thing went sour for him soon enough.

Slipping out of the last supper before the party was over, he led the way to the garden that he knew they were planning to adjourn to afterwards and said to lay low till he gave the signal. It was dark by the time his former associates showed up and maybe for fear that he might scare them off if he used any other method, the way he showed the soldiers which was the one to jump was by kissing him. That was all he'd been paid to do, and as soon as he'd done it, there was no earthly reason why he couldn't have taken off with his laundered cash and found a place to spend it. But when the time came, he wasn't in the mood.

There are several versions of what he did instead, of which the most psychologically plausible seems to be that he gave the money back to the ones who'd given it to him and went out and hanged himself. This time there doesn't seem to be any ambiguity about the motive.

There is a tradition in the early church, however, that his suicide was based not on despair but on hope. If God was just, then he knew there was no question where he would be heading as soon as he'd breathed his last. Furthermore, if God was also merciful, he knew there was no question either that in a last-ditch effort to save the souls of the damned as God's son, Jesus would be down there too. Thus the way Judas figured it, Hell might be the last chance he'd have of making it to Heaven, so to get there as soon as possible, he tied the rope around his neck and kicked away the stool. Who knows?

In any case, it's a scene to conjure with. Once again they met in the shadows, the two old friends, both of them a little worse for wear after all that had happened, only this time it was Jesus who was the one to give the kiss, and this time it wasn't the kiss of death that was given.

(John 12:1–8, 13:21–30, 18:1–12, Matthew 27:3–10)

JUDITH

King Nebuchadnezzar of Assyria (q.v.) had a nasty temper and a long memory, and after pulverizing his enemies the Medes, he sent a man named Holofernes with a hundred and thirty-two thousand men to straighten out all the peoples who hadn't coughed up military aid when he needed it. The ones who resisted were to be liquidated. The rest were to tear down their temples, throw out their gods, and see to it that from then on the only god they had any dealings with was Nebuchadnezzar himself.

The Jews were among the others on Nebuchadnezzar's black list, and the place where Holofernes attacked them was a town called Bethulia, to which he laid siege. In Bethulia there lived a very attractive, well-heeled young widow named Judith, and she decided to go to Holofernes and see what she could do.

First she prayed to Yahweh to prosper her cause and then, just to play it safe, made a few preparations of a more secular nature. She skinned out of the drab black clothes she'd been wearing in memory of her late husband and took a long, hot tub. Then she sprayed herself with some expensive *eau de cologne*, had her maid give her a permanent, and slipped into a dazzling little number left over from happier days. She polished things off by decorating herself with all the chains, bracelets, earrings, and assorted bric-a-brac she could put her hands on and set out with her maid for the enemy lines (Judith 10:1–5).

As a Jew, she had a little trouble getting to see Holofernes, but when she said she was going to show him how to take Bethulia without losing a single man, they let her in. "I will declare unto the Lord no lie this night," she told him as soon as they'd been introduced (Judith 11:6), and you can only hope she had her fingers crossed at the time.

The only circumstances under which Yahweh would think of letting his people be defeated, she said, was if they sinned. As it happened, she went on to say, right that minute they were sinning like crazy back in Bethulia by eating a lot of un-kosher food because, thanks to the siege, that was all there was left. She knew for a fact that the Jews in Jerusalem were about to pull the same stunt, and as soon as they did, Holofernes would be able to take the lot of them with both hands tied behind his back, and Yahweh wouldn't lift a finger to interfere. All Holofernes had to do was wait till she gave him the word.

Holofernes was not only much encouraged by what she had to say but knocked right off his pins by her good looks and fancy clothes. For three days he tried to lure her into his tent for an intimate little supper, and for three days she played hard to get. On the fourth day she finally said she'd come and put on an even flashier number for the occasion than the one she'd started out in. They had a gourmet meal together, during which Holofernes had three glasses of wine for every one of Judith's, and when it was over, he sent his servants packing so that it was just the two of them at last.

Unfortunately, he'd gotten himself so tanked up by then that before anything much had a chance to happen, he passed out on his bed. His scimitar was lying nearby, and with two good whacks Judith cut off his head, put it in her picnic basket, and went back to Bethulia, where she had it prominently displayed on the battlements. When the Assyrians saw it there the next day, they ran like rabbits, and the Jews drew their first easy breath in months.

They rewarded Judith by giving her the entire contents of Holofernes' tent including the silver cups and the bed he'd passed out on, but Judith turned around and gave them all to Yahweh. For all she knew, she might have forgotten to keep her fingers crossed when she said all those things to Holofernes the first time they met and thought the present might help make it up to Yahweh for having stretched things a little. And apparently she gauged things right because, although she never married again, she lived a long, happy life as Bethulia's leading citizen, and died peacefully in her bed at the age of one hundred and five.

(The Book of Judith)

Kk

KOHELETH

Koheleth means *preacher* and is the name by which the author of the Book of Ecclesiastes is known. When the rabbis got together to decide which books to put into the Old Testament and which to throw out, it is reported that Koheleth's almost didn't make it. You can't help seeing why, but at the same time you can't help being grateful to them for letting it in under the wire even so. In that great chorus of voices that speak out of the Bible, it is good to have this one long-drawn sigh of disillusion, skepticism, and ennui if only because the people who read the Bible sometimes feel that way themselves, not to mention also the ones who wouldn't be caught dead reading it.

People are born and people die, Koheleth says, and the sun goes up and the sun goes down, and first the wind blows from the north and then it blows from the south, and if you think you're seeing something for the first time, just go ask your grandmother, and if you think you're seeing something for the last time, just hang around for a while, and the whole thing is as pointless and endless and dull as a drunk singing all six dozen verses of *Roaming in the Gloaming* and then starting in from the beginning again in case you missed anything. There is nothing new under the sun, Koheleth says, with the result that everything that there is under the sun is both old and, as you might expect in all that heat, stinks.

If you decide to knock yourself out getting rich and living it up, he points out, all you have to show for it in the end is the biggest income tax in town and a bad liver; and when you finally kick the bucket, the chances are that your dim-witted heirs will sink the whole thing in a phony Florida real estate deal or lose it at the track in Saratoga. If you decide to break your back getting a decent education and end up a Columbia Ph.D. and an adviser to presidents, you'll be just as dead when the time comes as the high school drop-out who went into sausage-stuffing, and you'll be forgotten just about as soon.

If you decide to be Mr. Nice Guy and never do the dirty on a pal, that may rack you up some Brownie points somewhere, but it won't keep you from getting it in the teeth like everybody else because "there are righteous men to whom it happens according to the deeds of the wicked, and there are wicked men to whom it happens according to the deeds of the righteous," Koheleth says (Ecclesiastes 8:14), and we're all in the hands of God, all right, but "whether it is love or hate, man does not know" (Ecclesiastes 9:1).

God has a plan for us, to be sure, but he's left us in the dark as to what that plan is, and if God's plan happens to conflict with some we've made on our own, guess who gets his way? That is what the famous "A time to weep and a time to laugh" passage is all about (Ecclesiastes 3:1–9)—i.e., if you feel like laughing at a time which God has already pegged as a time for weeping, start reaching for the Kleenex.

"The race is not to the swift," he says, "nor the battle to the strong, nor bread to the wise, nor riches to the intelligent, nor favor to the men of skill" (Ecclesiastes 9:11), and that about sums it up. The dead are luckier than the living, he says, but luckiest of all are the ones who had the good sense never to get born in the first place.

But the rabbis in their wisdom let Koheleth into the Good Book anyway, placing him not far from the Psalms of David on one side and the Prophecies of Isaiah on the other. Maybe it was their hope that in that location a little of David and Isaiah might rub off on him, especially one of the insights they more or less shared which was that often people are closest to God when they need him most and that sometimes they know him best by missing him.

(The Book of Ecclesiastes)

KORAH

After years of knocking around the Promised Land with the children of Israel, Moses already had problems enough on his hands when some of his own people, led by a man named Korah, challenged his religious authority. "What makes you and your brother think you've got a corner on holiness?" Korah said and then added, "We're all holy, every last one of us." Moses was so undone by these remarks that, as the narrator reports, "he fell on his face" (Numbers 16:4).

He eventually picked himself up, however, and asked God to help him take care of these trouble-makers. God obliged by causing the ground to open up beneath their feet; Korah and his crowd were swallowed up and taken down alive to Sheol, the abode of the dead; and Moses was able to get on with the business of leading the way to the Promised Land.

You can't blame Moses for having overreacted the way he did. Leading the Israelites anywhere was no pushover, and he needed all the unchallenged authority he could get. On the other hand, you can't really blame Korah either, who, by insisting that nobody was any holier than anybody else, was simply anticipating by a few thousand years the doctrine of the priesthood of all believers.

As for God, there seems to be a strong possibility that the reason he caused the rebels to be swallowed down into Sheol *alive* was so that later on, when the whole thing had blown over, he could let them out again quietly through the back door.

(Numbers 16)

Ll

LABAN (*See* JACOB, RACHEL)

LAZARUS

Lazarus and his two sisters lived in a town called Bethany a couple of miles outside Jerusalem and according to the Gospel of John were among the best friends Jesus had. He used to drop in on them whenever he was in the neighborhood, and when he made his entrance into Jerusalem on Palm Sunday, it was from Bethany that he took off and it was also to Bethany that he went back to take it easy for a few days before his final arrest.

When Lazarus died, Jesus didn't arrive on the scene until several days afterwards, but he found the sisters still so broken up they hardly knew what they were saying. With one breath they reproached him for not having come in time to save their brother and with the next they told him they knew he could save him still. Then, for the first and only time such a thing is recorded of him in the New Testament, Jesus broke down himself. Then he went out to where his friend's body lay and brought him back to life again.

Recent interviews with people who have been resuscitated after being pronounced clinically dead reveal that after the glimpse they evidently all of them get of a figure of light waiting for them on the other side, they are very reluctant to be brought back again to this one. On the other hand, when Lazarus opened his eyes to see the figure of Jesus standing there in the daylight beside him, he couldn't for the life of him tell which side he was on.

(John 11:1–44)

LEAH (*See* RACHEL)

LOT

When God decided to wipe the city of Sodom off the map for its sins, he sent a couple of angels down to make sure that Lot was safely out of it first. Therefore he must have had something going for him. On the other hand, it's hard to see just what.

There was the way he conducted himself the day the angels arrived at his house, for instance. The first thing to happen was that some local weirdos started pounding on the front door demanding that he send the angels out to them for purposes which, though never spelled out, Lot seems to have understood well enough since, to save his guests, he immediately suggested that maybe they'd just as soon have his two unmarried daughters instead. The angels evidently thought this was going overboard on the laws of hospitality since before Lot had a chance to make good on his offer, they struck the door-pounders blind and sent them groping their way back to wherever they'd come from.

The next thing was that Lot went to the two young men who were engaged to his daughters, told them what the angels said was about to happen to Sodom, and advised them to pack their bags in a hurry. The two young men, who had presumably caught his act at the front door, refused to take him seriously. "They thought he was jesting," Genesis says (Genesis 19:14), and you can hardly blame them.

When the next morning arrived, Lot himself still hadn't gotten out of town, and the angels were in a snit. God had already started the countdown, and there wasn't a moment to lose. Lot refused to budge an inch, however, so finally in desperation the angels "seized him and his wife and his two daughters by the hand, the Lord being merciful to him, and they brought him forth and set him outside the city" (Genesis 19:16). Then they told him to flee to the hills before it was too late.

Lot's response must be read to be believed. "O no, my lords," he said. "Behold, your servant has found favor in your sight, and you have shown me great kindness in saving my life; but I cannot flee to the hills lest the disaster overtake me and I die. Behold, yonder city is near enough to flee to, and it is a little one. Let me escape there—is it not a little one?—and my life will be saved" Genesis 19:18–20).

All of Lot is somehow in that speech. To begin with, not so much as a passing thought is given to the imminent liquidation of all his fellow citizens. Beyond that, he knows perfectly well that he'll be safe in the hills or the angels would never have told him to go there, but wilderness camping isn't for him. He had already made it clear that he would rather be blown sky-high than leave and have to do without indoor plumbing, the morning paper delivered to the door, the restaurants. But he had a hunch the angels mightn't think all that highly of cities after their recent experience in one, so he tried to wheedle them as tactfully and unobtrusively as he could. Wouldn't it be all right if he fled just as far as that little city over there—that tiny little bit of a one you'd hardly even notice if you weren't looking straight at it? Just to get him moving, the angels gave him the nod, and by the time they'd finished giving it, he was already half way there.

His wife disobeyed the angels' instructions by looking back longingly at what they were leaving behind and was turned into a pillar of salt because of it. It was a dismal fate to be sure, but when you consider all the years of marriage to Lot that would probably have been in store for her otherwise, she may not have done all that badly at that.

(Genesis 19:1–29)

LUCIFER

Lucifer means *light-giver* or *morning star* or *son of dawn* and, ever since the Middle Ages, has been one of the aliases the Devil goes by along with Satan, Old Nick, Old Scratch, the Old Harry, and so forth. Thus the Bible's blackest villain is known by the Bible's loveliest name, and not by accident either.

"How art thou fallen from heaven, O Lucifer, son of the morning!" the prophet Isaiah says (Isaiah 14:12), the point being that it was while he was still at the height of his loveliness that the ugly episode took place.

Lucifer was a leading member of the heavenly chorus that sings Bach around the throne of grace and as such seemed so infinitely removed from all temptation that both to him and to all his fellow angels the very possibility must have seemed ludicrous. Then one day he made the mistake of saying to himself, "Just see how far I have come," with the emphasis on the first person singular, and from there to "Just see how far I can still go" was of course only a hop, skip, and a jump.

When you are one of God's right-hand men, there is clearly only one step further you can go, and with his usual uncanny combination of justice and mercy, God let him go there.

Lucifer was no longer called upon to love anybody except himself or to sing Bach anywhere but in the bathtub or to follow anything or anybody except his own instincts and inclinations. He was given an office with mottoes like *Nobody loves you like yourself* and *Nice guys finish last* on the walls and was named to the Number One job in charge of everybody else who both then and for all time felt the same way, and they have been having one Hell of a time together ever since.

LUKE

Of the four evangelists, Luke wrote the best Greek and, unlike the other three, was almost certainly a Greek-speaking Gentile himself who put his gospel together for a Gentile audience, translating Jewish names and explaining Jewish customs when he thought they wouldn't be understood if he didn't. In his letter to the Colossians, Paul refers to somebody as "Luke the beloved physician," and without stretching things too far, you could point to three blocks of material in Luke's gospel, omitted from the others, which might suggest that he was the same man.

First of all, there's the parable of the Prodigal Son, the account of the whore who washed Jesus's feet and dried them with her hair, and the scrap of conversation Jesus had with one of the two crooks who was crucified with him.

Smelling of pig and cheap gin, the prodigal comes home bleary-eyed and dead broke, but his father's so glad to see him anyway that he almost falls on his face. Jesus tells Simon the blue-nosed Pharisee that the whore's sins are forgiven her because even painted up like a cigar-store Indian and smelling like the perfume counter at the five and dime, she's got more in her of what the gospel of love is all about than the whole Ladies' Missionary Society laid end to end. The thief Jesus talked to on the cross may have been a purse-snatcher and second-story man from way back, but when he asked Jesus to remember him when he made it to where he was going, Jesus told him he'd make sure they got rooms on the same floor. Different as they all are in some ways, it's not hard to see that they all make the same general point, which is that though he could give them Hell when he felt like it, Jesus had such a soft spot in his heart for the scum of the earth that you would have almost thought he considered them the salt of the earth the way he sometimes treated them.

Second, Luke is the one who goes out of his way to make it clear how big Jesus was on praying. He prayed when he was baptized and after he healed the leper and the night before he called the twelve disciples, and Luke was the only one to mention these together with a few others like them and also was the only one to say that the last words Jesus ever spoke were the prayer, "Father, into thy hand I commend my spirit." It's also thanks to Luke that there's a record of the jokes Jesus told about the man who kept knocking at his friend's door till he finally got out of bed to open it and the widow who kept bugging the crooked judge till he finally heard her case just to get a little peace, the point of both of which seems to be that if you don't think God has heard you the first time, don't give up till you're hoarse. Luke wanted that to be remembered too.

Third and last, Luke makes sure that nobody misses the point that Jesus was always stewing about the terrible needs of poor people. He is the one who tells us that when Jesus preached at Nazareth, his text was "he has appointed me to preach good news to the poor" from Isaiah (Luke 4:18), and whereas Matthew says that the first beatitude was "Blessed are the poor in spirit," according to Luke it was just plain "Blessed are the poor" period (Luke 6:20). He also recorded some parables like the one about the rich man and the beggar which come right out and say that if the haves don't do their share to help the have-nots, they better watch out, and he's the only one to quote the song Mary sang which includes the words "he has filled the hungry with good things, and the rich has sent empty away" (Luke 1:53).

To put it in a nutshell, by playing all these things up Luke shows he was a man who believed that you shouldn't let the fact that a person is jail-bait keep you from treating him like a human being, and that if you pray hard enough, there's no telling what may happen, and that if you think you've got Heaven made but don't let it worry you that there are children across the tracks who are half starving to death, then you're kidding yourself. These characteristics may not prove that he was a doctor, like the Luke in Paul's letter, but if he wasn't, it was a serious loss to the medical profession.

Mm

MARK

Nobody knows for sure who wrote the gospel that bears Mark's name because the book itself doesn't say. Some people claim it was the John Mark who turns up in the Book of Acts as a traveling companion of Paul's and the son of a woman named Mary, who owned a place where the group used to meet and pray back in the days when the church was young (Acts 12:12). And maybe this John Mark was the same person who appears in the scene of Jesus's arrest at Gethsemane as a boy who managed to escape from the soldiers' clutches but not without leaving his shirt behind so that he ran off into the dark scared out of his wits and naked as the day he was born (Mark 14:51–52). Mark is the only one who reports the incident, and maybe he put it in as a kind of signature. An early historian says he was a friend of Peter's and got some of his information from him. Who knows? In the long run, the only things you can find out about him for certain are from the book he wrote. Whoever he was, Mark is as good a name to call him by as any other.

He was a man in a hurry, out of breath, with no time to lose because that's how the people were he was writing for too. The authorities were out for their blood, and they were on the run. At any moment of day or night a knock might come at the door, and from there to getting thrown to the lions or set fire to as living torches at one of Nero's evening entertainments took no time at all. So he leaves a lot out, it's amazing how much. There's no family tree for Jesus as there is in Matthew and Luke. There's nothing about how he was born, no angel explaining it ahead of time (*see* GABRIEL), no wise men, no Herod, no star. There's nothing about his childhood. There's precious little about his run-ins with the Pharisees, no Sermon on the Mount, only four parables. His teaching in general is brushed past hurriedly—except for one long speech, just a word here, a word there. "Immediately" is one of Mark's favorite words, and he uses it three times more than either Matthew or Luke, fifteen times more than John. "Immediately he called them" (1:20), "immediately on the sabbath he entered the synagogue" (1:21). Immediately the girl got up and walked (5:30), the father cried (9:24), the cock crowed (14:72). Jesus himself races by, scattering miracles like rice at a wedding. Mark is alive with miracles, especially healing ones, and Jesus rushes from one to another. He had no time to lose either.

Mark writes for people who already believe instead of the ones who need things explained, and therefore it's who Jesus was, rather than what he said, that Mark's book is bursting with—who he was and what he did with what little time he had. He was "the Son of God," that's who he was. Mark says it right out in the first sentence so nobody will miss it (1:1). And he came "not to be served but to serve, and to give his life as a ransom for many" (10:45). That's what he did, and he died doing it. The whole book is obsessed with the fact of his death. And with good reason.

If Jesus died as dead as anybody, what hope did the rest of them have who woke every morning to the taste of their own death in their mouths? Why did he die? He died because the Jews had it in for him, Mark says, because he is hard on the Jews, himself very likely a gentile and writing for Gentiles. He died because that's the way he wanted it—that "ransom for man" again, a wonderful thing to be bought at a terrible price. He died because that's the way God wanted it. Marvelous things would come of his death, and the one long speech Mark gives has to do with those marvelous things. "The stars will be falling from Heaven," Jesus says, "and the powers in the heavens will be shaken, and then they will see the Son of Man coming in clouds with great power and glory" (13:26–27). Of course there was hope—hope that would set the stars reeling like drunks at a fair.

But even in the midst of his great haste, Mark stops and looks at Jesus, *sees* him better than any of the others do. When Jesus naps in a boat, it's in the *stern* he does it, with a *pillow* under his head (4:38). The others don't say that. And the grass was *green* when he fed the five thousand on hardly enough to feed five (6:39), not dry grass, crackling and brown. He got up "a great while before day" to go pray by himself (1:35), not at nine, not after a hot breakfast, and he was sitting down "opposite the treasury" when he saw the old lady drop her two cents in the collection box (12:41). Only Mark reports how the desperate father said, "I believe. Help thou my unbelief" (9:24), and how Jesus found it belief enough to heal his sick boy by. You can say they make no difference, such details as these which the others skip, or you can say they make all the difference.

Then the end comes, and even Mark has to slow down there. Half his book has to do with the last days in Jerusalem and the way Jesus handled them and the way he was handled himself. And when he died, Mark is the one who reports what his last words were, even the language he spoke them in—*Eloi, Eloi, lama sabachthani*—which he translates, "My God, my God, why hast thou forsaken me?" (15:34). Only Matthew had the stomach to pick them up from Mark and report them too. Luke and John apparently couldn't bring themselves to.

Mark ends his book, as he begins it, almost in the middle of a sentence. There was no time to gather up all the loose ends. The world itself was the loose ends, and all history would hardly be enough to gather them up in. The women went to the tomb and found it empty. A young man in white was sitting there—"on the right," Mark says, not on the left. "He has risen," the young man said. "Go tell his disciples. And Peter," Mark adds, unlike Matthew and Luke again. Was it because he'd known Peter and the old man had wanted his name there? So the women ran out as if the place was on fire, which in a way of course it was, "for trembling and astonishment had come upon them, and they said nothing to anyone for they were afraid" (16:1–8). Later editors added a few extra verses to round things off, but that's where Mark ended it. In mid-air.

Mark's last word in his gospel is *afraid,* and it makes you wonder if maybe the theory is true after all that he was the boy who streaked out of Gethsemane in such a panic. He knew how the women felt as they picked up their skirts and made a dash for it anyway. Wonderful and terrible things were happening, and more were still to come. He knew what fear was all about—the scalp cold, the mouth dry, the midnight knock at the door—but he also knew that fear was not the last thing. It was the next to the last thing. The last thing was hope. "You will see him, as he told you," the young man in white said (16:7). If that was true, there was nothing else that mattered. So Mark stopped there.

MARY (*See also* GABRIEL)

The time their twelve-year-old got lost in Jerusalem and they finally found him in the Temple, Mary said, "Behold, thy father and I have sought thee sorrowing" (Luke 2:48), and as things turned out, it was a shadow of things to come.

It's not hard to imagine her sorrowing again when Jesus left a good, steady job in Nazareth to risk his neck wandering around all over creation to proclaim whatever it was he thought he was proclaiming. Part of her sorrow was presumably that she loved him too much for himself instead of for the wild and holy business he thought he'd been called to. Another part must have been that like just about everybody else who was closest to him in Nazareth, she never really understood what he thought he was doing and may well have been one of the ones who, when he went back home once, decided he must be off his rocker. "He is beside himself," they said (Mark 3:21) and tried to lock him up for his own good.

Maybe some of the things he said to her didn't sound as bad in Aramaic as they do in English, but even so she can't have been too happy about the time she told him the wine was running out at the wedding in Cana, and he said, "Woman, what have you to do with me?" (John 2:4) or the time they came and told him his mother was waiting outside for him, and he said, "Who is my mother?" (Matthew 12:48), adding that whoever did the will of his father who was in heaven, that was who his mother was.

For all the sentimentalizing that their relationship has come in for since, there's no place in the Gospels where he speaks some special, loving word or does some special, loving thing for the woman who gave him birth. You get the idea that he felt he couldn't belong truly to anybody unless he somehow belonged equally to everybody. They were all his mothers and brothers and sisters, and there's no place in the record where he offers her anything more than he offered everybody else.

No place, that is, except at the very end when, cross-eyed with pain, he looked down from where they'd nailed him and said something just for her. Even here he didn't call her his mother, just "woman" again, and he didn't say goodbye to her or anything like that. But it's as if here at last he finally spoke to the awful need he must have always sensed in her. "Behold your son," he said, indicating the disciple who was standing beside her, and then to the disciple, "Behold your mother" (John 19:26–27).

It was his going-away present to her really, somebody to be the son to her that he had had no way of being himself, what with a world to save, a death to die. He would be present in that disciple, he seemed to be saying, for her to live for, and to live for her. Beyond that, he would be present in generation after generation for her to mother, the Mater Dolorosa who seeks him always, and sorrowing, everywhere she goes.

MARY MAGDALENE

It is sometimes held that Mary Magdalene was the woman Luke tells about whom, to the righteous horror of Simon the Pharisee, Jesus let wash his feet and dry them with her hair despite her highly unsavory reputation, and about whom Jesus said, "I tell you, her sins, which are many, are forgiven because she loved much" (Luke 7:47). It's a powerful story, and it would be nice to think that Mary Magdalene is the one it's about, but unfortunately there's no really good reason for doing so.

When Jesus was on the road with his disciples, he had a group of women with him whom he'd cast evil spirits out of once and who had not only joined up with him but all chipped in to help meet expenses. One of them was Mary Magdalene, and in her case it was apparently not just one evil spirit that had been cast out but seven. Just what her problem had been, nobody says, but helped along by the story in Luke, tradition has it that she'd been a whore. Maybe so. In any case, she seems to have teamed up with Jesus early in the game and to have stuck with him to the end. And beyond.

It's at the end that she comes into focus most clearly. She was one of the women who was there in the background when he was being crucified—she had more guts than most of them had—and she was also one of the ones who was there when they put what was left of him in the tomb. But the time that you see her best was on that first Sunday morning after his death.

John is the one who gives the greatest detail, and according to him it was still dark when she went to the tomb to discover that the stone had been rolled away from the entrance and that, inside, it was empty as a drum. She ran back to wherever the disciples were hiding out to tell them, and Peter and one of the others returned with her to check out her story. They found out that it was true and that there was nothing there except some pieces of cloth the body had been wrapped in. They left then, but Mary stayed on outside the tomb someplace and started to cry. Two angels came and asked her what she was crying about, and she said, "Because they have taken away my lord, and I do not know where they have laid him" (John 20:13). She wasn't thinking in terms of anything miraculous, in other words; she was thinking simply that even in death they wouldn't let him be and somebody had stolen his body.

Then another person came up to her and asked the same questions. Why was she crying? What was she doing there? She decided it must be somebody in charge, like the gardener maybe, and she said if he was the one who had moved the body somewhere else, would he please tell her where it was so she could go there.

Instead of answering her, he spoke her name—Mary—and then she recognized who he was, and though from that in-

stant forward the whole course of human history was
changed in so many profound and complex ways that it's impossible to imagine how it would have been different otherwise, for Mary Magdalene the only thing that had changed
was that for reasons she was in no state to consider, her old
friend and teacher and strong right arm was alive again, and
RABBONI! she shouted and was about to throw her arms
around him for sheer joy and astonishment when he stopped
her.

Noli me tangere, he said. *Touch me not. Don't hold on to me*
(John 20:17), thus making her not only the first person in
the world to have her heart stop beating for a second to find
him alive again when she'd thought he was dead as a doornail but the first person also to have her heart break a little to
realize that he couldn't be touched any more, wasn't there
any more as a hand to hold onto when the going got tough, a
shoulder to weep on, because the life in him was no longer a
life she could know by touching it, with her here and him
there, but a life she could know only by living it: with her
here—old tart and retread, old broken-heart and last, best
friend—and with him here too, alive inside her life, to raise
her up also out of the wreckage of all that was wrecked in
her and dead.

In the meanwhile, he had much to do and far to go, he
said, and so did she, and the first thing she did was go back
to the disciples to report. "I have seen the Lord," she said,
and whatever dark doubts they might have had on the subject earlier, one look at her face was enough to melt them all
away like morning mist.

(John 20:1–18)

MATTHEW

The apostle Matthew was a tax-collector, and one of the
gospels bears his name. Like Mark's, the book was written
anonymously and the name attached to it later. Maybe it
contains some of Matthew's recollections buried in it some-

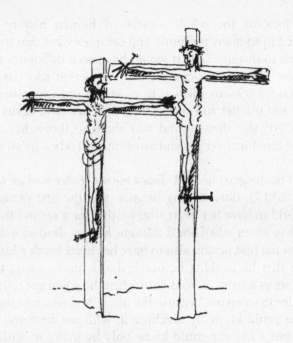

where. Maybe not. In any case, it's the man who wrote it who's of chief interest here, and all we know about him is what his book tells us. He didn't write it from scratch but included virtually all of Mark in it plus a collection of the sayings of Jesus that seems to have been floating around plus some other material peculiar to him. It's what he did with it all that tells the kind of man he was.

What he did with it especially was to show that if, on the one hand, faith in Jesus was as new as a newborn babe, on the other hand it was as old as the hills. As very likely a Jew himself, Matthew knew his Torah, and according to him, Jesus was what the Torah was all about whether anybody knew it or not. Much of his life was foretold there, Matthew keeps saying, and he loved to give examples. "Behold, a virgin shall conceive and bear a son, and his name shall be called Emmanuel," the prophet Isaiah had said, and Matthew nailed his idea that Mary was a virgin to that (1:23). Jesus was born at Bethlehem, and that's just where the prophet Micah had said he'd be born (2:6). Hosea was the one who predicted the flight into Egypt when Jesus was still on his mother's knee (2:15), and it was Zechariah who said he'd come riding into Jerusalem on a donkey like a king great in his humbleness and humble in his greatness (21:5). But things like this were mere window-dressing compared with the main thing Matthew wanted to say.

The main thing he wanted to say was that although Jesus was born in the sticks and never had two cents to rub together and was ignored by just about everybody who mattered and was strung up in the end between two crooks, he was the same Messiah, the same Christ, the same Anointed of the Lord, that for centuries Israel had been waiting for with tears in its eyes. Everything Matthew wrote was aimed at convincing people that this was so and that to accept it was to find eternal life and that to deny it was to be like the Pharisees to whom Jesus said, "Woe to you . . . sons of those who murdered the prophets . . . you serpents, you brood of vipers, how are you to escape being sentenced to Hell?" (23:29–33). Nobody loved the Jews more than Matthew did, writing till he was blue in the face so they would believe and be saved, but nobody was harder on them either. It was Matthew who added to Mark's account the terrible words they spoke when Pilate washed his hands of the whole grim business: "His blood be on us and on our children" (27:25).

Jesus was the Messiah, Matthew said, and he was also a second Moses, giving his sermon on the mount just as Moses had brought the tablets down from Mt. Sinai but taking the fierce old stone and making pure gold of it. "You have heard that it was said 'An eye for an eye and a tooth for a tooth,' but I say to you, do not resist one who is evil" (5:38–39). "You have heard that it was said, 'You shall love your neighbors and hate your enemies,' but I say to you, love your enemies and pray for those who persecute you" (5:43–44). As Matthew saw it, Jesus came not to drown the old law out, as the Jews supposed, but to make it sing new, like an angel.

It worried him a little the way in Mark's gospel the Son of God sometimes sounds so much like anybody's son, and he did what he could to patch things up. Where Mark wrote that when Jesus healed the leper, he was "moved with pity" (Mark 1:41), Matthew leaves out the pity and says he just healed him. When Mark says he looked at the people who objected to miracles on the Sabbath "with anger, grieved at their hardness of heart" (Mark 3:5), Matthew leaves that out too. He won't let him "sigh deeply" when they ask him for a sign (Mark 8:12), and Mark's "he could do no mighty work" in his own hometown (Mark 6:5) becomes just "he did not" do any in Matthew (13:58). "Why do you call me good? No one is good but God alone," Jesus says in Mark to the man who greets him that way (Mark 10:18), and Matthew tinkers with it till it reads, "Why do you ask me about what is good?" (19:17). You can't blame him for tinkering really. He can't help retouching the photograph when he loves its subject so—making the warts a little less wartlike, the miracles a little more miraculous—and in the end he lets him at least die like a man as well as like a God with the same dark cry that Mark reports—"My God, my God, why have you let me down?" (27:46).

Mark ends his gospel with the women tearing out of the empty tomb in terror. Things were happening beyond their power to cope with, "and they said nothing to any one, for they were afraid" (Mark 16:8). But in Matthew the angel tells them not to be. "Don't be afraid," he says (28:5). There was no reason to be afraid, Matthew says. It was all set down right there in the Torah if you just knew how to read it right. Hadn't Isaiah written, "He will not wrangle or cry aloud, nor will any one hear his voice in the streets; he will not break a bruised reed or quench a smouldering wick"? (12:19–20).

Such a man as that, so gentle and kind, was bound to come to such an end. There was no need to be afraid. And yet wasn't it written also, "The people who sat in darkness have seen a great light, and for those who sat in the region of the shadow of death, light has dawned"? (4:16). Dawned for the gentle man himself, and for the frightened women, and dawned for everyone else too who would only hear and believe.

The women took the angel's word to heart apparently because though "they departed quickly from the tomb with fear," Matthew says, they departed also with "great joy" and ran to tell the disciples what had happened because they couldn't hold it in any longer (28:8). And just in case there should be any question as to what their great joy was all about, Matthew ends his gospel with words that explain it. "Lo, I am with you always," Jesus says, "even unto the end of the world" (28:20), and for once Matthew felt that no Old Testament reference was necessary.

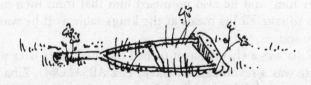

MEPHIBOSHETH

Mephibosheth was only five years old when news came through that his father, Jonathan, and his grandfather, King Saul, had both been killed in battle. Terrified of what might happen next, his nurse snatched him up in her arms and started to run off with him when she tripped and fell in her panic, and the boy was so badly crippled that he never walked right again.

The new king, David, might very well have decided to get rid of him. It was standard procedure then to wipe out your predecessor's entire family when you came to the throne just in case any of them happened to have political ambitions; but maybe because Mephibosheth was a cripple and thus not likely to give him much trouble, or maybe because his father had been David's best friend, or maybe just because he felt sorry for him or some combination of all these, David decided to be generous. It was the kind of crazy, magnificent gesture he liked to make every once in a while, like the time some soldiers risked their necks breaking through the enemy lines to bring him a cup of cool water from Bethlehem, his home-town, and David won the hearts of everybody by saying, "Shall I drink the blood of the men who went at the risk of their lives?" (2 Samuel 23:15–17), and poured it out on the ground.

In any case, he had Mephibosheth brought to him, and the poor child fell on his face in terror at what for all he knew was going to be the axe, but David told him not to be afraid. He told him that he was to have all the property that rightfully belonged to him and a man named Ziba to look after him, and he also promised him that from then on he was to take all his meals at the king's table as if he was his own son.

Ziba was a sly one, as it turned out, and years later when there was a revolt against David (*see* ABSALOM), Ziba told him that Mephibosheth had defected to the other side. What motivated this lie was the hope that David would grant him not only his favor but also all Mephibosheth's real estate, and so David did.

After the revolt was successfully put down, however, Mephibosheth showed up and convinced David that Ziba had been lying and he had been on the right side all along, and David seemed to believe him. But poor David—he was so shattered by everything that had happened, especially by the death of his beloved if treacherous Absalom, (q.v.) that he couldn't give the matter his full attention and more or less brushed Mephibosheth off by telling him that he and Ziba could divide the real estate between them for all he cared and to stop pestering him.

It would be sad if the relationship had ended on such an unsatisfactory note—the old king too broken-hearted to care much about anything any more, and Mephibosheth limping home to work things out somehow with Ziba. But that isn't where it ended.

Before David had a chance to leave, Mephibosheth said that he was so overjoyed that David had driven the rascals out and come through the battle safe and sound that just to celebrate he was prepared to let Ziba take the whole damn place. Whether or not he made good on the offer, or even intended to, hardly matters. It was a crazy and magnificent gesture to make, and maybe David was not too lost in his own grief to realize, however dimly, at whose feet he had learned to make it.

(2 Samuel 9, 16:1–4, 19:24–30)

MICAH

When Micah's mother discovered the silver missing, the last person she suspected was her son Micah so she laid a curse on the unknown thief's head that was enough to fell an ox. This threw such a scare into Micah that he produced the silver from under his bed and owned up.

To show there were no hard feelings, his mother counter-acted the curse with a blessing that was enough to make hair grow on a doorknob. She also said she wanted Micah to have the money anyway since he seemed to want it so badly but told him to use it in a good cause. What he did was to have it melted down into a religious statue that made the Golden Calf look like an animal cracker and hired a priest just to take care of it. He had the idea that not only was this a good cause but it was also good business. "Now I know that the Lord will prosper me," he said (Judges 17:13). That's what he knew.

After a while a bunch of Danite toughs turned up who were so impressed by the silver statue they decided they'd have to have it. The priest started to make a fuss as they were struggling out the door with it, but when they explained to him that working for a tribe like the Danites got you a lot more in the way of fringe benefits than working for one small-time crook with an Oedipus complex, his scruples were overcome, and they ended up getting not only the statue but the priest to go with it.

Micah chased after them, of course, and accused them of grand larceny. In his heart he knew he was hardly the one to talk, however, and his tone of righteous indignation sprang some visible leaks. "What ails you?" the Danites said (Judges 18:24), casually fingering their cartridge belts, and Micah suddenly remembered a previous engagement.

In addition to such basic lessons as *Honesty is the best policy* and *The pot shouldn't call the kettle black,* it is to be hoped that Micah also learned that God, unlike Mother, wasn't to be bought off with a mumbled apology motivated entirely by fear and a pious offering by Van Cleef and Arpels.

(Judges 17–18)

MORDECAI (*See* XERXES)

MOSES

Whenever Hollywood cranks out a movie about him, they always give the part to somebody like Charlton Heston with some fake whiskers glued on. The truth of it is he probably looked a lot more like Tevye the milkman after ten rounds with Mohammed Ali.

Forty years of tramping around the wilderness with the Israelites was enough to take it out of anybody. When they weren't raising Hell about running out of food, they were raising it about running out of water. They were always hankering after the fleshpots of Egypt and making bitter remarks about how they should have stayed home and let well enough alone. As soon as his back was turned, they started whooping it up around the Golden Calf (*see* AARON), and when somebody stood up and said he ought to be thrown out, the motion was seconded by thousands (*see* KORAH). Any spare time he had left after taking care of things like that he spent trying to persuade God not to wipe them out altogether as they deserved.

And then, of course, there was the hardest blow of all. When he finally had it all but made and got them as far as the top of Mt. Pisgah, where the whole Promised Land stretched out before them as far as the eye could see, God spoke up and said this was the place all right, but for reasons which were never made entirely clear, Moses was not to enter it with them. So he died there in his one hundred and twentieth year, and after a month of hanging around and wishing they'd treated him better, the Israelites went on in without him.

Like Abraham before him and Noah before that, not to mention like a lot of others since, the figure of Moses breathing his last up there in the hills with his sore feet and aching back serves as a good example of the fact that when God puts the finger on people, their troubles have just begun.

And yet there's not a doubt in the world that in the last analysis Moses, like the rest of those tough old birds, wouldn't have had it any different. Hunkered down in the cleft of a rock once, with God's hand over him for added protection, he had been allowed to see the Glory itself passing by, and although all God let him see was the back part, it was something to hold on to for the rest of his life. And then there was one other thing that was even better than that.

Way back when he was just getting started and when out of the burning bush God had collared him for the first time, he had asked God what his name was, and God had told him so that from then on he could get in touch with him any time he wanted. Nobody had ever known God's name before Moses did, and nobody would ever have known it afterwards except for his having passed it on; and with that thought in his heart up there on Pisgah, and with that name on his lips, and with the sunset in his whiskers, he became in the end a kind of burning bush himself.

Nn

NAAMAN

Naaman was a five-star general in the Syrian army and also a leper. His wife had working for her a little Jewish slave-girl who mentioned one day that there was a prophet named Elisha (q.v.) back home who could cure leprosy as easily as a toad cures warts. So Naaman took off for Israel with a letter of introduction from the king and a suitcase full of cash and asked Elisha to do his stuff.

Elisha told him to go dunk in the Jordan seven times, and after some initial comments to the effect that there were rivers back in Syria that made the Jordan look like a cow track, Naaman went and did what he was told. When he came out, he could have passed for an ad for Palmolive soap. Naaman was so grateful that he converted on the spot and reached into his suitcase for an inch of fifties, but Elisha said he was a prophet of Yahweh, not a dermatologist, and refused to take a cent.

Elisha had a servant named Gehazi, however, who had different ideas. He hot-footed it after Naaman and told him that Elisha had changed his mind. He said that if Naaman would like to make a small contribution to charity, he, Gehazi, would make sure it got into the right hands. Naaman was only too pleased to hand over the inch of fifties, and Gehazi went home and deposited it in his personal checking account.

When Elisha got wind of it, he told Gehazi that the healing power of God was not for sale to the highest bidder and to press his point home transferred Naaman's leprosy to him. For the sake of Naaman's newfound faith in Yahweh as above all a God of love and mercy, it would be nice to believe that news of Elisha's overreaction never reached him in Syria.

(2 Kings 5)

NAOMI (*See* RUTH)

NATHAN

Just about every king seems to have had a prophet to be a thorn in his flesh and help keep him honest. Saul had Samuel, Ahab had Elijah, Hezekiah had Isaiah, Jehoiachim and Zedekiah seem to have shared Jeremiah, and so on. King David was the one who had Nathan. There is nothing of Nathan's in writing so it's impossible to grade him on literary skill, but when it comes to the ability to stick the stiletto in with maximum efficiency, he gets a straight A. The best example is, of course, the most famous.

David had successfully gotten rid of Uriah the Hittite by assigning him to front-line duty where he was soon picked

off by enemy snipers. After a suitable period of mourning, David then proceeded to marry Uriah's gorgeous young widow, Bathsheba. The honeymoon had hardly started rolling before Nathan came around to describe a hardship case he thought David might want to do something about.

There were these two men, Nathan said, one of them a big-time rancher with flocks and herds of just about everything that has four legs and a tail and the other a small-time subsistence type with just this one lamb he was too soft-hearted even to think about in terms of chops and mint jelly. He had it living at home with himself and the kids, and he got to the point where he even let it lap milk out of his own cereal bowl and sleep at the foot of his bed. Then one day the rancher had a friend drop in unexpectedly for a meal and, instead of taking something out of his own overstuffed freezer, got somebody to go over and commandeer the poor man's lamb which he and his friend consumed with a garnish of roast potatoes and new peas.

When Nathan finished, David hit the roof. He said anybody who'd pull a stunt like that ought to be taken out and shot. At the very least he ought to be made to give back four times what the lamb was worth. And who was the greedy, thieving slob anyway, he wanted to know.

"Take a look in the mirror the next time you're near one," Nathan said. It was only the opening thrust. By the time Nathan was through, it was all David could do just to pick up the receiver and tell Room Service to get a stiff drink up to the bridal suite.

(2 Samuel 12:1–15)

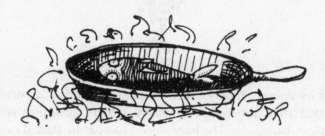

NATHANIEL

Philip could hardly wait to tell somebody, and the first person he found was Nathaniel. Ever since Moses they'd been saying the Messiah was just around the corner, and now, by God, if he hadn't finally turned up. Who would have guessed where? Who would have guessed who?

"Jesus of Nazareth," Philip said. "The son of Joseph." But he could hear his words fall flat even as he was saying them. It wasn't as if he'd said it was the head rabbi or somebody.

"Can anything good come out of Nazareth?" Nathaniel said. Or Podunk maybe? *Brooklyn?*

Philip told him to come take a look for himself then, but Jesus got a look at Nathaniel first as he came puffing down the road toward him, near-sighted and earnest, with his yarmulke on crooked, his dog-eared Torah under his arm.

"Behold, an Israelite indeed, in whom is no guile," Jesus said. Nathaniel was sweating like a horse. His thick specs were all fogged up. His jaw hung open. He said, "How do you know me?" His astonishment made him stammer.

"Before Philip called you," Jesus said. "when you were under the fig tree, I saw you."

It was all it took apparently. "Rabbi!" Nathaniel's jacket was too tight across the shoulders and you could hear a seam split somewhere as he made an impossible bow. "You are the Son of God," he said. "You are the King of Israel."

"Because I said I saw you under the fig tree, do you believe?" Jesus said. There was more to it than parlor tricks. He said, "You shall see greater things than these." But all Nathaniel could see for the moment, not daring to look up, were his own two sneakers, pigeon-toed in the dust.

"You will see heaven opened," he heard Jesus say, "the angels of God ascending and descending upon the Son of Man." When Nathaniel decided to risk a glance, the sun almost blinded him.

What Nathaniel did see finally was this. It was months later, years. One evening he and Peter and a few of the others took the boat out fishing. They didn't get a nibble between them but stuck it out all night. It was something to do anyway. It passed the time. Just at dawn, in that queer half-light, somebody showed up on the beach and cupped his mouth with his hands. ANY LUCK? The answer was No in more ways than one, and they said it. Then give it another try, the man said. Reel in the nets and cast them off the starboard beam this time. There was nothing to lose they hadn't lost already so they did it, and the catch had to be seen to be believed, had to be felt, the heft of it almost swamping them as they pulled it aboard.

Peter saw who the man was first and heaved himself overboard like a side of beef. The water was chest-high as he plowed through it, tripping over his feet in the shallows so he ended up scrambling ashore on all fours. Jesus was standing there waiting for him by a little charcoal fire he had going. Nathaniel and the others came ashore, slowly, like men in a dream, not daring to speak for fear they'd wake up.

Jesus got them to bring him some of their fish, and then they stood around at a little distance while he did the cooking. When it was done, he gave them the word. "Come and have breakfast," he said, and they all came over and sat down beside him in the sand.

Nathaniel's name doesn't appear in any of the lists of the twelve apostles, but there are many who claim he was also known as Bartholomew, and that name does appear there. It would be nice to think so. On the other hand, he probably considered it honor enough just to have been on hand that morning at the beach, especially considering the unfortunate remark he'd made long ago about Nazareth.

They sat there around the fire eating their fish with the sun coming up over the water behind them, and they were all so hushed and glad and peaceful that anybody passing by would never have guessed that, not long before, their host had been nailed up on a hill outside the city and left there to die without a friend to his name.

(John 1:43–51, 21:1–14)

NEBUCHADNEZZAR (See also DANIEL, JUDITH)

Nebuchadnezzar, King of Babylon, was a real horror. The ingenuities of his torture chamber made those of Vlad the Impaler look like paddle tennis. When King Zedekiah of Israel rebelled against him, for instance, he had his eyes put out—which anybody could have thought of—but the master-touch was that just before this was done, he had Zedekiah's sons killed before him in some appropriately loathsome way so that in his blindness he'd have that last sight to live with for the rest of his days.

And then there was the famous trio of Shadrach, Meshach, and Abednego. They were all three of them employees of the Babylonian civil service, but as Jews they believed there was one God only, and his name was Yahweh. Therefore when Nebuchadnezzar had a ninety-foot idol made out of 18-karat

gold and commanded everybody to grovel at its feet Or Else, Shadrach, Meshach, and Abednego tried to get themselves registered as conscientious objectors. Nebuchadnezzar lost no time in ordering them to be thrown into a flaming, fiery furnace prepared especially for the occasion.

He ordered the furnace to be heated to seven times its normal temperature, had the three trussed up in their long black overcoats, galoshes, and derby hats, and then took his seat in the front row center. The fire was so hot that the men who tossed them in were burned to a crisp in the process. This wasn't supposed to be part of the act, and neither was what happened next. First of all, Nebuchadnezzar could see that there were four men in the furnace instead of three and that the fourth was an angel. Second, they were all obviously fireproof.

Nebuchadnezzar was so undone that he called to them to come out, and when they emerged with not even their earlocks singed, he pardoned them on the spot and remarked that Yahweh was clearly a God you didn't fool around with. He then went a step further by issuing a new command to the effect that from that day forward, anybody caught treating Yahweh with anything but the highest respect was to be torn limb from limb and have his house burned down, in that order.

Yahweh was presumably pleased by this sudden conversion of Nebuchadnezzar's, but he may have had the sense that there were still a few rough edges to take care of before the job was complete.

(Daniel 3, 2 Kings 25:7)

apples

NEHEMIAH

Nehemiah broke down and wept when he found out that the walls of Jerusalem were still in ruins from when the Babylonians had pulled them down over a century earlier. The Persians had replaced the Babylonians as the number one superpower by then, and, as luck would have it, Nehemiah was one of the King of Persia's right-hand men. So, waiting till the king was in a mellow mood after his second planter's punch, he went and asked for permission to go home to Jerusalem and supervise its refortification. The king said not to stay too long but gave him the go-ahead anyway.

To strengthen his hand when he got to Jerusalem, he even had him made governor.

It took Nehemiah twelve years to get the job done, and it was tough sledding all the way. The Samaritans thought he was rebuilding the walls to keep them out and so did their friends. Others made a fuss because they were suspicious of a Jewish governor who worked for Persia. A man named Tobiah said that any wall Nehemiah was likely to build would fall to pieces the first time a fox stubbed his toe on it (Nehemiah 4:3). The construction crews threatened to walk off the job because back on the farm what the weeds hadn't taken over, the neighbors had. The Jerusalem Jews tended to be free-and-easier about religion than Nehemiah was so they objected to him as a narrow-minded, holier-than-thou Puritan prude. And so on. But after twelve years the walls somehow got put back in working order anyway, Nehemiah threw a big celebration, and then he went back to Persia.

After another twelve years, he showed up in Jerusalem to see how things had been getting on and almost had a heart attack. The walls were strong as ever, but inside the walls everything had gone to pot. Tobiah, the man who'd made the remark about the fox, was living like a king in the Temple while a lot of priests were out on the street corners selling apples. Everybody went to work on the Sabbath just like any other day, and all the big stores were open, not to mention the bars, and if people bothered to go to church at all, they could hardly hear the service over the spiel of the Tyrian fish-peddlers. Worst of all in Nehemiah's eyes, there were a lot of Jewish boys who'd not only married foreign girls but had picked up their foreign ways to such an extent that most of their kids didn't even know Hebrew.

Once again Nehemiah rose to the occasion. He tossed Tobiah out on his ear and had the place fumigated. He took the priests off the streets. He reinstated the Blue Laws with a vengeance. He sent the fish-peddlers packing. He had the city gates locked from Saturday night till Monday morning. As for the boys who'd married wrong, he reminded them how even the great Solomon had gotten into trouble over his taste for imported cheesecake, and to make sure they wouldn't forget, he "contended with them and cursed them and beat some of them and pulled out their hair" (Nehemiah 13:25). By the time he was through, he had Jerusalem looking like a convention of Hard-Shell Baptists.

The ones who called Nehemiah a blue-nosed Puritan weren't entirely off-base, of course, but you can't help admiring him anyway. It's too bad that one of his favorite prayers had to be "Remember for my good, O my God, all that I have done for this people" (Nehemiah 5:19, compare 13:14, 31). It would be nice to think he'd done it all for love. But even when he went wrong, he went wrong for the right reasons mostly, and when his time finally came, it's at least ten to one that God didn't fail to remember.

(The Book of Nehemiah)

NICODEMUS

Nicodemus had heard enough about what Jesus was up to in Jerusalem to make him think he ought to pay him a visit and find out more. On the other hand, as a VIP with a big theological reputation to uphold, he decided it might be just as well to pay it at night. Better to be at least fairly safe than to be sorry, he thought, and waited till he thought his neighbors were all asleep.

So Nicodemus was fairly safe, and, at least at the start of their nocturnal interview, Jesus was fairly patient. What the whole thing boiled down to, Jesus told him, was that unless you got born again, you might as well give up.

That was all very well, Nicodemus said, but just how were you supposed to pull a thing like that off? How especially were you supposed to pull it off if you were pushing sixty-five? How did you get born again when it was a challenge just to get out of bed in the morning? He even got a little sar-

castic. Could a man "enter a second time into his mother's womb," he asked (John 3:4), when it was all he could do to enter a taxi without the driver's coming around to give him a shove from behind?

A gust of wind happened to whistle down the chimney at that point, making the dying embers burst into flame, and Jesus said being born again was like that. It wasn't something you *did*. The wind did it. The Spirit did it. It was something that happened, for God's sake.

"How can this be?" Nicodemus said (John 3:9), and that's when Jesus let him have it.

Maybe Nicodemus had six honorary doctorates and half a column in *Who's Who*, Jesus said, but if he couldn't see something as plain as the nose on his face, he'd better go back to kindergarten.

"I'm telling you like it is," Jesus said. "I'm telling you what I've seen. I'm telling you there are people on Medicare walking around with the love-light in their eyes. I'm telling you there are ex-cons teaching Sunday School. I'm telling you there are undertakers scared silly we'll put them out of business."

Jesus said, "I'm telling you God's got such a thing for this loused-up planet that he's sent me down so if you don't believe your own eyes, then maybe you'll believe mine, maybe you'll believe me, maybe you won't come sneaking around scared half to death in the dark any more but will come to, come clean, come to *life*."

What impressed Nicodemus even more than the speech was the quickening of his own breathing and the pounding of his own heart. He hadn't felt like that since his first pair of long pants, his first kiss, since the time his first child was born or the time they'd told him he didn't have lung-cancer but just a touch of the flu.

Later on, when Jesus was dead, he went along with Joseph of Arimathea (q.v.) to pay his last respects at the tomb in broad daylight. It was a crazy thing to do, what with the witch-hunt that was going on, but he decided it was more than worth it.

When he heard the next day that some of the disciples had seen Jesus alive again, he wept like a newborn baby.

(John 3:1–21, 19:38–42)

NOAH (*See also* HAM)

The waters had all drained off and the ground was dry again when God hung a rainbow in the sky to remind him he'd promised "that never again shall all flesh be cut off by the waters of a flood" (Genesis 9:11). The way he explained it to Noah, "I will look upon it and remember the everlasting covenant between God and every living creature that is upon the earth" (Genesis 9:13).

In one way, then, it gave Noah a nice warm feeling to see the rainbow up there, but in another way it gave him an uneasy twinge. If God needed the rainbow as a reminder, he thought, that could mean that if someday God didn't happen to look in the right direction or had something else on his

mind, he might forget his promise and the heavy drops would start pattering down on the roof a second time.

Noah could never forget the first time—how little by little the waters had risen, first just spreading in over the kitchen linoleum and trickling down the cellar stairs but eventually floating newspapers and pictures off tables and peeling wallpaper off walls until people were driven to the rooftops where they sat wrapped in blankets with their transistor radios on their laps looking up for a break in the clouds and reassuring each other that this must be the clearing shower at last. He remembered the animals he'd had to leave behind—the old sow with her flaxen lashes squealing on top of a hen house as the ripples lapped at her trotters, the elephants awash up to their hips, a marmalade cat with one ragged ear clinging to a TV aerial as a pair of parakeets in a wicker cage floated by over what had once been the elementary school gym.

He also remembered the endless days on the ark—the miserable food, the sea-sickness, the smells. When the downpour finally stopped, he sent birds out to see if they could find any dry land anywhere, and he remembered watching them fly away until they were no bigger than flyspecks on a windowpane, remembered the feeling in his stomach when they finally flew back having found no place to roost.

He remembered especially one of the doves and how, when he saw it returning, he had reached out over the rail, and it had landed on the callouses of his upturned palm. With his eyes closed and tears on his cheeks, he had touched his lips to its feathers, and as he felt the panic of its bird's heart, it had seemed to him that the whole world was just as fragile and as doomed.

But then, after weeks, another dove came back with a sprig of olive in its beak, and the tops of the mountains began to reappear out of the watery waste, and now at last the great, glittering rainbow arched above him, and the great promise echoed in his ears. "Never again," God had said, and Noah clung on to those words like a raft in a high sea.

With the rainbow tied around his little finger to jog his memory, surely God would never forget what he'd said. No matter what new meanness men might think up, surely the terrible thing would never happen again. As an expert in hoping against hope, the old sailor told himself that the worst was over and that as sure as God made little green apples, a new, green world would blossom up out of the sodden wreckage of the old.

He then planted the first vineyard and invented wine. The way he figured it, wine would help him forget the dark past and, if all went well, would be like the champagne at a wedding that you toast the future with. And if all did not go well, if doubts and fears began to gather like rain clouds in his heart, then wine would help him ride out the storm within as before he'd ridden out the forty days and forty nights.

In the meantime, he would keep his eye on the rainbow and his hand near the corkscrew and try to be fruitful and multiply just the way God had told him and his seven-time great-grandfather Adam before him.

(Genesis 6–9)

Oo

ONAN

The ancient law was that if a man died, his brother was supposed to have a child by his widow so the line wouldn't become extinct. Therefore, when Er died, it was up to his brother Onan to perform the duty with Er's widow, Tamar. Because Onan knew that the child to be born wouldn't really be his, he refused and "spilled his semen on the ground" instead (Genesis 38:9). As a result, God killed him.

This story is dismal enough in itself, but later generations have made it more so. Onanism has become a euphemism for masturbation, and the punishment Onan received has been interpreted as meaning that God is, to say the least,

141

against it. Actually what God was against was that Onan had disobeyed the law of levirate marriage and had done so on the unedifying grounds that he didn't want any children of his running around with another man's name. Presumably the punishment would have been just as severe if, instead of doing what he did, he'd simply caught the next bus out of town.

According to Dr. Kinsey, some 92 percent of all males have masturbated and some 62 percent of all women. The only damage to come of it seems to be the crippling sense of guilt and terror inculcated by well-meaning, pious folk who, forgetting their own sexual past, say that it makes you go crazy or blind or have your hair fall out.

There seem to be no Scriptural grounds for condemning masturbation in itself. Like sex in general, if it is practiced to the exclusion of a loving relationship with other human beings, it is an infraction of the law of love and is its own punishment. On the other hand, if it's practiced as a temporary expedient until the right person comes along, it is harmless. It was not for his sexuality that Onan was punished but for his stinginess and selfishness and general cussedness.

(Genesis 38:1–10)

ONESIMUS

Saint Paul was serving one of his periodic sentences behind bars when he met Onesimus. Onesimus was a slave who belonged to a Christian friend named Philemon, and why he was in jail nobody knows. Maybe he was a runaway. Maybe Philemon had charged him with theft. Anyway, when Onesimus had done his stretch and was about to be sprung, Paul wrote a short letter for him to give to his master, Philemon, when he got back home.

While they were doing time together, Paul wrote, not only had he made a Christian out of Onesimus but he had also made him one of his best friends. The boy was like a son to

him, Paul said, and sending him back was like "sending my very heart" (Philemon 1:12). *Onesimus* means "useful," and Paul plays on the name by saying he's become so useful to him that he doesn't know what he'll do without him. He doesn't come right out and say what he wants Philemon to do, but the hint could hardly be broader. "I would have been glad to keep him with me in order that he might serve me on your behalf during my imprisonment for the Gospel," he wrote, "but I preferred to do nothing without your consent." In case that wasn't enough, he added, "Yes, my brother, I want some benefit from you in the Lord. Refresh my heart in Christ." In the meanwhile he hopes that Philemon will receive the boy back "no longer as a slave but more . . . as a beloved brother" (Philemon 1:13–20).

It's not known whether or not Philemon took the hint and let Onesimus return to be the old saint's comfort for what time was left him, but there's at least one good reason for believing that such was the case. Years later, when Paul was long since dead, another saint by the name of Ignatius was in jail. The Bishop of Ephesus had sent some friends to visit him, and Ignatius wrote asking if a couple of them could be allowed to stay. Ignatius in his letter used some of the same language that Paul had used in his to Philemon, almost as if he was trying to remind him of something. And what was the name of the Bishop he wrote to? It was Onesimus.

There's no proof that he was the same slave-boy grown old and venerable with a mitre on his head, but it's very tempting to believe so. If he was, then he refreshed the hearts of not just one old saint but two, and was more true to his name, *useful*, than Paul ever lived to discover.

(Philemon. *See also* John Knox, *Philemon Among the Letters of Paul*, University of Chicago Press, 1935)

Pp

PAUL (*See also* AGRIPPA, EUTYCHUS, FELIX, ONESIMUS, STEPHEN)

He wasn't much to look at. "Bald-headed, bowlegged, strongly built, a man small in size, with meeting eyebrows, with a rather large nose." Years after his death that's the way the apocryphal *Acts of Paul and Thecla* describes him, and Paul himself quotes somebody who had actually seen him: "His letters are strong, but his bodily presence is weak" (2 Corinthians 10:10). It was no wonder.

"Five times I have received at the hands of the Jews the forty lashes less one," he wrote. "Three times I have been beaten with rods. Once I was stoned. Three times I have been shipwrecked. A night and a day I have been adrift at sea. In danger from rivers . . . robbers . . . my own people . . .

Gentiles. In toil and hardship, in hunger and thirst . . . in cold and exposure" (2 Corinthians 11:24–27). He also was sick off and on all his life and speaks of a "thorn in the flesh" that God gave him "to keep me from being too elated" (2 Corinthians 12:7). Epilepsy? Hysteria? Who knows? The wonder of it is that he was able to get around at all.

But get around he did. Corinth, Ephesus, Thessalonica, Galatia, Collossae, not to mention side trips to Jerusalem, Cyprus, Crete, Malta, Athens, Syracuse, Rome—there was hardly a whistle-stop in the Mediterranean world that he didn't make it to eventually, and sightseeing was the least of it. He planted churches the way Johnny Appleseed planted trees. And whenever he had ten minutes to spare he wrote letters. He bullied. He coaxed. He comforted. He cursed. He bared his soul. He reminisced. He complained. He theologized. He inspired. He exulted. Punch-drunk and Christ-drunk, he kept in touch with everybody. The postage alone must have cost him a fortune, not counting the energy and time. And where did it all start? On the road, as you might expect. He was still in charge of a Pharisee goon squad in those days and was hell-bent for Damascus to round up some trouble-making Christians and bring them to justice. And then it happened.

It was about noon when he was knocked flat by a blaze of light that made the sun look like a forty-watt bulb, and out of the light came a voice that called him by his Hebrew name twice. "Saul," it said, and then again "Saul. Why are you out to get me?" and when he pulled himself together enough to ask who it was he had the honor of addressing, what he heard to his horror was, "I'm Jesus of Nazareth, the one you're out to get." We're not told how long he lay there in the dust then, but it must have seemed at least six months. If Jesus of Nazareth had what it took to burst out of the grave like a guided missile, he thought, then he could polish off one bowlegged Christian-baiter without even noticing it, and Paul waited for the axe to fall. Only it wasn't an axe that fell. "Those boys in Damascus," Jesus said. "Don't fight them, join them. I want you on my side," and Paul never in his life forgot the sheer lunatic joy and astonishment of that moment. He was blind as a bat for three days afterwards, but he made it to Damascus anyway and was baptized on the spot. He was never the same again, and neither, in a way, was the world (Acts 9:1–6, 22:4–16, 26:9–18).

Everything he ever said or wrote or did from that day forward was an attempt to bowl over the human race as he'd been bowled over himself while he lay there with dust in his mouth and road apples down the front of his shirt: *Don't fight them, join them. He wants you on his side.* YOU, of all people. ME. Who in the world, who in the solar system, the galaxy, could ever have expected it? He knew it was a wild and crazy business—"the folly of what we preach," he said—but he preached it anyway. "A fool for Christ's sake" he called himself as well as weak in his bodily presence, but he knew that "the folly of God was wiser than the wisdom of men and the weakness of God was stronger than men" (1 Corinthians 1:18–25). There were times he got so carried away that his language went all out of whack. Infinitives split like atoms, syntax exploded, participles were left dangling.

"By grace you have been saved," he wrote to the Ephesians, and *grace* was his key word. GRACE. Salvation was free, *gratis.* There was nothing you had to do to earn it and nothing you *could* do to earn it. "This is not your own doing, it is the gift of god—not because of works, lest any man should boast," and God knows he'd worked, himself, and boasted too—worked as a Pharisee, boasting about the high marks he'd racked up in Heaven till the sweat ran down and Christian heretics dropped like flies—only to find en route to Damascus that he'd been barking up the wrong tree from the start, trying to beat and kick his way through a door that had stood wide open the whole time. "For we are *his* workmanship, created in Christ Jesus for good works," he wrote; in other words, good works were part of it, all right, but after the fact, not before (Ephesians 2:8–10).

Little by little the forgiven person became a forgiving person, the person who found he was loved became capable of love, the slob that God had had faith in anyway became de-slobbed, faithful, and good works blossomed from his branches, from her branches, like fruit from a well-watered tree. What fruit? Love, Paul wrote the boys and girls in Galatia. Love was the sweetest and tenderest. And then "joy, peace, patience, kindness, goodness, faithfulness, gentleness, self-control" till his typewriter ribbon was in tatters and he had to take to a pencil instead (Galatians 5:22–23).

And Christ was his other key word, of course. CHRIST— the key to the key. He never forgot how he'd called him by name—twice, to make sure it got through—and "while we were yet sinners, Christ died for us," he wrote out for the Romans (Romans 5:6) and for the Galatians again, "I have been crucified with Christ"—all that was dried up in him, full of hate and self-hating, self-serving and sick, all of it behind him now, dead as a doornail—so that "it is no longer I who live but Christ who lives in me" (Galatians 2:20). And then, to the Philippians by registered mail, return receipt requested: "For me to live is Christ" (Philippians 1:21), and to the Ephesians, for fear they'd feel neglected if the mailman came empty-handed, "You he made alive when you were dead" (Ephesians 2:1). Alive like him.

But there were other times too. Sometimes the depression was so great he could hardly move the pencil across the page. "I don't understand my own actions," he said. "For I don't do what I want, but I do the very thing I hate. . . . I can will what is right, but I can't do it. For I don't do the good I want but the evil I don't want is what I do. . . . For I delight in the law of God in my inmost self, but I see in my members another law at war with the law in my mind and making me captive to the law of sin. . . . Wretched man that I am! Who will deliver me from this body of death?" He sat there by himself, aiming his awful question at the plaster peeling off his walls, and maybe it was only ten minutes or maybe it was ten years before he had the heart to scratch out the answer: "Thanks be to God through Jesus Christ our Lord," he said (Romans 7:15–25).

It got him going again, and on the next page he was back in his old stride with a new question. "If God is for us, who is against us?" He worked on that one for a minute or two and then gave it another try. "Who shall separate us from the love of Christ? Shall tribulation, or distress, or persecution, or famine, or nakedness, or peril, or sword?" It was the story of his life, needless to say, and at last he'd laid the ground for an answer he could get his back into. "NO!" he wrote, the tip of his pencil-point breaking off, he bore down so hard. "In all these things we are more than conquerors through him who loved us. For I am sure that neither death, nor life, nor angels, nor principalities, nor things present, nor things to come, nor powers, nor height, nor depth, nor anything else in all creation, will be able to separate us from the love of God in Christ Jesus our Lord" (Romans 8:31–39). He sat there with his cauliflower ear and a lump on his forehead the size of an egg from the last time the boys had worked him over, and when he reached for the drawer to get out an envelope, he found that his hand was shaking so badly he could hardly open it.

The ups and the downs. The fights with his enemies and the fights with his friends. The endless trips with a fever and diarrhea. Keeping one jump ahead of the sheriff. Giving his spiel on windy street corners with nobody much to hear him most of the time except some underfed kids and a few old women and some yokels who didn't even know the language. Where was it all going to get him in the end? Where was it all going to get all of them, any of them, in the end?

When you came right down to it, what was God up to, for God's sweet sake, sending them all out—prophets, apostles, evangelists, teachers, the whole tattered bunch—to beat their gums and work themselves into an early grave?

God was making a body for Christ, Paul said. Christ didn't have a regular body any more so God was making him one out of anybody he could find who looked as if he or she might just possibly do. He was using other people's hands to be Christ's hands and other people's feet to be Christ's feet, and when there was some place where Christ was needed in a hurry and needed bad, he put the finger on some maybe-not-all-that-innocent bystander and got him to go and be Christ in that place himself for lack of anybody better.

And how long was the whole great circus to last? Paul said, why, until we all become *human beings* at last, until we all "attain to mature manhood," as he put it; and then, since there had been only one really *human* being since the world began, until we all make it to where we're like him, he said— "to the measure of the stature of the fullness of Christ" (Ephesians 4:11–13). Christs to each other, Christs to God. All of us. Finally. It was just as easy, and just as hard, as that.

Nobody's sure whether he ever got to Spain the way he'd planned or not, but either before he went or soon after he got back, he had his final run-in with the authorities, and the story is that they took him to a spot about three miles out of Rome and right there on the road, where he'd spent most of his life including what was in a way the beginning of his life, they lopped off his head.

At the end of its less than flattering description of his personal appearance, the *Acts of Paul and Thecla* says that "at times he looked like a man, and at times he had the face of an angel." If there is a God in Heaven, as even in his blackest moments Paul never doubted there was, then bald-headed and bowlegged as he was, with those eyebrows that met and that over-sized nose, it was with angel eyes that he exchanged a last long glance with his executioners.

PETER (*See also* ANANIAS, MARK)

Everybody knows he started out as a fisherman. He lived with his wife in Capernaum, where they shared a house with his mother-in-law and his brother Andrew. He and Andrew had their own boat and were in business with a couple of partners named James and John, Zebedee's sons. The first time Jesus laid eyes on him, he took one good look and said, "So you're Simon, the son of John" (John 1:42), and then said that from then on he'd call him Cephas, which is Aramaic for Peter, which is Greek for *rock*.

A rock isn't the prettiest thing in creation or the fanciest or the smartest, and if it gets rolling in the wrong direction, watch out, but there's no nonsense about a rock, and once it settles down, it's pretty much there to stay. There's not a lot you can do to change a rock or crack it or get under its skin, and, barring earthquakes, you can depend on it about as much as you can depend on anything. So Jesus called him the Rock, and it stuck with him the rest of his life. Peter the Rock. He could stop fishing for fish, Jesus told him. He'd been promoted. From there on out people were to be his business. Now he could start fishing for them.

There was a lot of talk going around about who Jesus was and who he wasn't, and Jesus himself seemed just as glad to steer clear of the subject. Then one day he brought it up himself, and the disciples batted it around for a while. There were some people who said he was John the Baptist come back from the grave, they told him, or maybe Elijah, or Jeremiah, or some other prophet who thought he'd see what he could do a second time around. There were all kinds of half-baked theories, they said. Then Jesus put it to them straight: "Who do YOU say that I am?" Nobody wanted to stick his neck out, and the silence was deafening till Peter broke it or till it washed up against the rock that Peter was and broke itself. "You're the Christ," he said, "the Son of the living God" (Matthew 16:15–16).

It took a lot of guts to say, and Jesus knew it did. If it was true, it was enough to blow the lid off everything. If it wasn't true, you could get yourself stoned to death as a blasphemer for just thinking it. But Peter said it anyway, and Jesus made up for him the only beatitude he ever made up for a single individual and said, "Blessed are you, Simon Bar-Jona," which means Simon, son of John, and seems to have been what he always called him when he really meant business. Then he went back to Peter the Rock again and told him that he was the rock he wanted to build his church on and that as soon as he got to Heaven, he was to be the one to decide who else got in. "I will give you the keys of the kingdom," Jesus said (Matthew 16:17–19). It was another promotion.

But if Peter was the only one Jesus ever gave a beatitude of his own to, he was also the only one he ever gave Hell to, at least in quite such a direct way. It happened not long afterwards. Jesus was saying that to be the Christ, the Son of the living God, wasn't going to be a bed of roses all the way, and the time wasn't far off when he'd suffer the tortures of the damned in Jerusalem and be killed. Peter couldn't take it. "God forbid, Lord. This shall never happen," he said, and that's when Jesus lit into him. "Get behind me, Satan," he said because the rock that Peter was at that point was blocking the grim road that Jesus knew he had to take whether he or Peter or anybody else wanted it that way or not because God wanted it that way, and that was that. "You're not on God's side but men's," he said. "You're a rock I've cracked my shins on" (Matthew 16:21–23).

It wasn't the last time Peter said the wrong thing either, or asked the wrong question, or got the wrong point, or at least failed to do the thing that was right. The day he saw Jesus walking on the water and tried to walk out to him himself, for instance, he was just about to go under for the third time because rocks have never been much good at floating when Jesus came to the rescue (Matthew 14:28–31). Once when Jesus was talking about forgiveness, Peter asked how many times you were supposed to forgive any one person—seven times maybe?—and Jesus turned on him and said that after you'd forgiven him seventy times seven you were just starting to get warmed up (Matthew 18:21–22). Another time Jesus was talking about Heaven, and Peter wanted to know what sort of special deal people like himself got, people who'd left home and given everything up the way he'd given everything up to follow Jesus; and Jesus took it easy on him that time because a rock can't help being a little thick sometimes and said he'd get plenty, and so would everybody else (Matthew 19:27–30).

And then there were the things he did or failed to do, those final, miserable days just before the end. At their last supper, when Jesus started to wash the disciples' feet, it was Peter who protested—"*You* wash *my* feet!"—and when Jesus explained that it showed how they were all part of each other and servants together, Peter said, "Lord, not my feet only but my hands and my head!" and would probably have stripped down to the altogether if Jesus hadn't stopped him in time (John 13:5–11). At that same sad meal, Jesus said he would have to be going soon, and because Peter didn't get what he meant or couldn't face it, he asked about it, and Jesus explained what he meant was that he was going where nobody on earth could follow him. Peter finally got the point then and asked *why* he couldn't follow. "I'll lay down my life for you," he said, and then Jesus said to him the hardest thing Peter had ever heard him say. "Listen, listen," he said, "the cock won't crow till you've betrayed me three times" (John 13:36–38), and that's the way it was, of course—Peter sitting out there in the high priest's courtyard keeping warm by the fire while, inside, the ghastly interrogation was in process, and then the girl coming up to ask him three times if he wasn't one of them and his replying each time that he didn't know what in God's name she was talking about. And then the old cock's wattles trembling scarlet as up over the horizon it squawked the rising sun, and the tears running down Peter's face like rain down a rock (Matthew 26:69–75).

According to Paul, the first person Jesus came back to see after Easter morning was Peter. What he said and what Peter said nobody will ever know, and maybe that's just as well. Their last conversation on this earth, however, is reported in the Gospel of John.

It was on the beach, at daybreak. Some of the other disciples were there (*see* NATHANIEL), and Jesus cooked them breakfast. When it was over, he said to Peter (only again he called him Simon, son of John, because if ever he meant business, this was it), "Simon, son of John, do you love me?" and Peter said he did. Then Jesus asked the same question a second time and then once again, and each time Peter said he loved him—three times in all, to make up for the other three times.

Then Jesus said, "Feed my lambs. Feed my sheep," and you get the feeling that this time Peter didn't miss the point (John 21:9–19). From fisher of fish to fisher of people to keeper of the keys to shepherd. It was the Rock's final promotion, and from that day forward he never let the head office down again.

PHILEMON (See ONESIMUS)

PHILIP (See ETHIOPIAN EUNUCH, NATHANIEL, SIMON MAGUS)

PILATE (See also HEROD ANTIPAS)

As the Roman governor, Pilate had the last word. He could have saved Jesus if he'd wanted to, and all indications are that for various reasons that's what he'd like to have done.

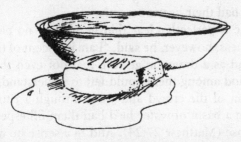

In the first place, after personally interrogating him, he decided that no wrong had been done and said so. "I find no crime in this man," he told the chief priests. Period (Luke 23:4). Maybe the man had committed some religious *faux pas* in their eyes, but the religion of the Jews was nothing to him, and he couldn't have cared less. In fact, as a sophisticated Roman, religion in general was not his cup of tea, and he'd been quite frank about it to Jesus himself during their interview. When Jesus told him he'd come to bear witness to the truth, Pilate's reply was "What is truth?" (John 18:38). Truth was for people who had time to worry about truth. Pilate was a busy man. In the second place, on the basis of a troubling dream she'd had, Pilate's wife begged him "to have nothing to do with that righteous man" (Matthew 27:19), and, sophisticated or not sophisticated, that gave him pause. A woman's intuition was not something you sneezed at, especially if you happened to be married to her. In the third place, his main job as a colonial administrator was to keep peace in the colonies at any price, and the last thing he wanted to do was to stir up a hornet's nest by making a martyr out of some local hero.

Nevertheless, when it became clear that he would stir up an even nastier hornet's nest by setting the man free, and when, in addition to that, the Jews pointed out that no true friend of Caesar's would ever be soft on a man who had set himself up as a king to rival Caesar, Pilate prudently gave in to the pressures and said to go ahead and crucify him if that's what they had their hearts set on.

To make it perfectly clear that he wanted no part in the dirty business, however, he said, "I am innocent of this man's blood," and as a dramatic gesture that not even the dullest colonial clod among them could fail to understand, stepped out in front of the crowd and went through a ritual handwashing in a basin of water he'd had them fill especially for that purpose (Matthew 27:24). And in a sense he was right. Insofar as he'd done all he reasonably could to save the man—even offering to let them crucify Barabbas (q.v.) instead if it was just a show they were after—he was, in a manner of speaking, innocent. The crucifixion took place against his advice and better judgment.

In this connection, you can't help thinking about that other famous hand-washer, Lady Macbeth. Unlike Pilate, Lady Macbeth had committed murder herself, and what she kept trying to wash away in her sleep, long after her hands themselves were clean as a whistle, was her tormenting sense of guilt over the terrible thing she had done. She never succeeded, of course, but God is merciful, and one can hope that in the long run he did the job for her.

Pilate's case is different and worse. For him, it was not so much the terrible thing he'd done as the wonderful thing he'd proved incapable of doing. He could have stuck to his guns and resisted the pressure and told the chief priests to go to Hell, where they were obviously heading anyway. He could have spared the man's life. Or if that is asking too much, he could have spared him at least the scourging and catcalls and the appalling way he died. Or if that is still asking too much, he could have spoken some word of comfort when there was nobody else in the world with either the chance or the courage to speak it. He could have shaken his hand. He could have said goodbye. He could have made some two-bit gesture which, even though it would have made no ultimate difference, to him would have made all the difference.

But he didn't do it, he didn't do it, and on that basis alone you can almost believe the sad old legend is true that again and again his body rises to the surface of a mountain lake and goes through the motion of washing its hands as he tries to cleanse himself not of something he'd done, for which God could forgive him, but of something he might have done but hadn't, for which he could never forgive himself.

(Matthew 27:15–26)

Qq

QUEEN OF SHEBA

The Queen of Sheba decided to go see for herself if King Solomon was all he was cracked up to be, and, court etiquette being what it was, she didn't go empty-handed. She brought enough camels to stock six zoos and gold and jewels enough to fill a dozen steamer trunks and so many spices that when the wind blew the wrong way, it almost knocked you off your feet. She also anointed herself from head to toe with Chanel No. 5, fastened on herself as many feathers, ribbons, and diamonds as there were places to fasten them, and when she arrived in Jerusalem, it was like a Mardi Gras parade.

Since part of what Solomon was famous for was his skill at riddles, she brought a number of those along too. *Which came first, the chicken or the egg?* and *What goes up a chimney down but won't go down a chimney up?* were among the easier ones, and the others were real shin-crackers. Solomon knocked them all off one right after another without even batting an eye and said it was like shooting fish in a barrel. He then offered to give her a guided tour of the palace.

He showed her wine cellars that made her feathers tremble with excitement and storerooms full of marvelous things to eat that had her mouth watering all over her upper diamonds. He showed her his personal wardrobe, remarking that most of it was last season's stuff, and the uniforms of all his butlers, bodyguards, chambermaids, and cupbearers, together with an estimate of what it cost per year just to have them dry-cleaned. He showed her a dining-room table that could seat the whole State Department down to the last under-secretary's secretary, plus the gold plates he used when he wanted to put on the dog and the massive silver service he kept for when he wanted just a quiet evening at home with the family. When he took her to the place where he kept burnt offerings for Yahweh, she thought they'd wandered into the Chicago stockyards by mistake. By the time they'd finished, the Queen was so undone that she had to excuse herself and go to her room, where she took off her girdle, put her feet up, and had her lady's maids apply cold compresses until the bell rang for supper. As the Book of Kings sums it up, "There was no more spirit in her" (1 Kings 10:5).

After supper she rallied enough to make a little speech. Seeing was believing, she said, but she still thought her contact lenses must need readjustment. She'd heard plenty before she came, but she now knew she hadn't heard the half of it. She couldn't say which he was better at, cracking riddles or picking wives, and the fifty of them or so who were present because they weren't pregnant at the time applauded politely. She said Yahweh must be tickled pink to have a king like Solomon on the payroll. Then she sat down, but not before making him a bread-and-butter present of as much of the gold and jewels and spices and camels as she thought she wouldn't be needing herself on the trip home.

Solomon responded by giving her so much in return that it made what she'd given him look like something she'd picked up at a tag sale, and when she got back to Sheba, it was some years before she ventured forth again.

(1 Kings 10:1–13)

QUIRINIUS

Saint Luke says that Jesus was born in the year "when Quirinius was governor of Syria" (Luke 2:2) whereas it is indicated elsewhere that at the same time Herod the Great (q.v.) was king. Since Quirinius wasn't governor until ten years or so after Herod was dead, the two dates can't really be reconciled although for centuries scholars eager to defend Scriptural accuracy in all things have knocked themselves out trying to reconcile them.

So maybe Luke made a mistake. The inspiration of the Scriptures is no more undermined by the fact that their chronology isn't infallible than the inspiration of Shakespeare is undermined by the fact that he thought there was a sea-coast in Bohemia.

(Luke 2:2)

Rr

RACHEL

The life of Jacob's wife Rachel was never an easy one. In the first place, she had Laban for a father, and in the second place, she had Jacob for a husband. And then, of course, she also had her sister Leah.

Rachel was the younger and prettier of the two girls, and Laban told Jacob that if he worked hard for seven years for him, he could have her. So Jacob worked hard for seven years, but when the wedding night rolled around at last, Laban sneaked Leah in in Rachel's place, and it wasn't till Jacob got a good look at her the next morning that he realized he'd been had. Leah was a nice girl, but she had weak eyes, and Rachel was the one he'd lost his heart to anyway.

161

Laban gave some kind of shaky explanation about how it was an old family custom for the oldest daughter to get married first no matter what, and Jacob had to work another seven years before Rachel was finally his in addition to Leah.

To be married to two sisters simultaneously is seldom recommended even under the best of circumstances, and in this case it was a disaster. For a long time Rachel couldn't have babies, and Leah had four. When they weren't fighting with each other, they were fighting with Jacob, and when Jacob wasn't fending them off, he was trying to out-cheat his crooked father-in-law (*see* JACOB) with the result that in the end the whole situation blew up, and Jacob cleared out with both his wives plus Laban's household gods which Rachel pinched for luck just as they were leaving because luck was what she felt she was running out of. It wasn't long afterwards that Rachel died on the road giving birth to a son whom she lived just long enough to name Benoni, which means "Son of my sorrow," although Jacob changed it to Benjamin later on.

Even in death her problems weren't over. From her sons and Leah's the twelve tribes of Israel descended, and the whole story of the Old Testament is basically the story of how for years to come they were always getting into one awful mess after another with God, with their neighbors, and with themselves. Centuries later, when the Babylonians carried them off into exile, it was Jeremiah (q.v.) who said that even in her tomb she was grieving still. "A voice is heard in Ramah, lamentation and bitter weeping," he said. "Rachel is weeping for her children" (Jeremiah 31:15).

But Rachel's children were also God's children, according to Jeremiah, and the last words were God's too. "Is Ephraim my dear son?" God said, naming one of them to stand for them all. "Is he my darling child?" And then God answered his own question in a way that even to Rachel, with her terrible luck, must have brought some hope. "Therefore my heart

yearns for him," God said, "and as often as I speak against
him, I do remember him still" (Jeremiah 31:20).

(Genesis 29–31, 35)

RAHAB

Rahab ran an unpretentious little establishment in the
red-light district of Jericho and was known for, among other
things, her warm and generous heart. That is perhaps why,
when Joshua was getting ready to attack, the spies he sent in
to case the joint made a bee-line for her.

When the King of Jericho found out they were there, he
rang Rahab up and over the din of the piano player downstairs managed to get it across to her who they were and that
she was to turn them in on the double if not quicker. Rahab
replied that though it was true some customers answering
his description had been there that evening, she'd thought
they were just a couple of butter-and-egg men out for a good
time and had kissed them goodbye not more than twenty

minutes earlier. If he got a move on, he could probably still catch them.

She then went up to the roof where she had the spies stashed away and told them what had happened. She said that as far as she was concerned, the customer was always right, and she had no intention of squealing on them. She also said she felt it in her bones that with Yahweh on his side, Joshua was going to find Jericho a pushover when the attack began. All she asked in return for her services was that when the boys came marching in, they'd give her and her family a break.

The spies were only too happy to agree, she let them down with a rope, and they beat it back to headquarters to report to Joshua. A few days later, when Joshua went through Jericho like a dose of salts, he saw to it that Rahab and her family got out before he burned the place down, and they lived happily ever after.

Matthew lists Rahab as one of the ancestresses of the Lord Jesus Christ (Matthew 1:5), and that may be one reason why there was something about free-wheeling ladies with warm and generous hearts that he was never quite able to resist.

(Joshua 2, 6)

REBECCA

Rebecca's marriage to Isaac was a family arrangement rather than a love-match, and all the love she had in her to give she seems to have lavished on her son Jacob.

When she overheard old Isaac say that he was going to give Jacob's twin brother, Esau, the paternal blessing and make him his heir, she was almost beside herself. She ran and told Jacob what was up and said he'd better get to Isaac before Esau did or Esau would get the blessing and everything that went with it and Jacob wouldn't get a blessed thing. Jacob objected that blind as Isaac was, he would still be able to tell the brothers apart because Esau was a hairy

man whereas he, Jacob, had all he could do just to raise a toothbrush moustache. Just one touch, Jacob said, and the old duffer would know that something fishy was going on (*see* ISAAC).

Rebecca thought fast and, after dressing Jacob up in one of Esau's best suits, produced some bearskin gloves for him to put on his hands and an extra pelt to wrap around his neck. The trick worked beautifully. Isaac thought it was Esau kneeling before him, and Jacob carried the day.

When the cat was finally out of the bag, Esau first burst into tears and then announced that by the time he got through with Jacob, not even his mother would recognize him. But again Rebecca thought fast. She told Jacob what his brother had in mind and persuaded him to get out of town while he could still walk. Jacob took the advice, and the bitter irony of it is that if Rebecca ever saw the apple of her eye again, it is at least not so recorded.

It is also not recorded when or where or in what state of mind Rebecca finally died, but there is a note to the effect that when the time came, they buried the lonely old woman in a cave at Machpelah. Years later Jacob was buried there too, and if she had any way of knowing about it, one can imagine her happy at last to be lying there side by side with the beloved boy for whose sake she had betrayed not only Isaac, her husband, and Esau, her son, but God himself, in whose name the fateful blessing had been given.

(Genesis 24–27)

RUTH

Ruth was a Moabite girl who married into a family of Israelite transplants living in Moab because there was a famine going on at home. When her young husband died, her mother-in-law, Naomi, decided to pull up stakes and head back for Israel where she belonged. The famine was over by then, and there was no longer anything to hold her where she was, her own husband having died about the same time that Ruth's had. She advised Ruth to stay put right there in Moab and to try to snag herself another man from among her own people.

She was a strong-willed old party, and when Ruth said she wanted to go to Israel with her, she tried to talk her out of it. Even if by some gynecological fluke she managed to produce another son for Ruth to marry, she said, by the time he was old enough, Ruth would be ready for the geriatric ward. But Ruth had a mind of her own too, besides which they'd been through a lot together what with one thing and another, and home to her was wherever Naomi was. "Where you go, I go, and where you live, I live," Ruth told her, "and if your God is Yahweh, then my God is Yahweh too" (Ruth 2:10–17). So Naomi gave in, and when the two of them pulled in to Bethlehem, Naomi's hometown, there was a brass band to meet them at the station.

Ruth had a spring in her step and a fascinating Moabite accent, and it wasn't long before she caught the eye of a well-heeled farmer named Boaz. He was a little long in the tooth, but he still knew a pretty girl when he saw one, and before long, in a fatherly kind of way, he took her under his wing. He told the hired hands not to give her any trouble. He helped her in the fields. He had her over for a meal. And when she asked him one day in her disarming Moabite way why he was being so nice to her, he said he'd heard how good she'd been to Naomi, who happened to be a distant cousin of his, and as far as he was concerned, she deserved nothing but the best.

Naomi was nobody's fool and saw which way the wind was blowing long before Ruth did. She was dead-set on Ruth's making a good catch for herself, and since it was obvious she'd already hooked old Boaz whether she realized it or not, all she had to do was find the right way to reel him in. Naomi gave her instructions. As soon as Boaz had a good supper under his belt and had polished off a nightcap or two, he'd go to the barn and hit the sack. Around midnight, she said, Ruth should slip out to the barn and hit the sack too. If Boaz's feet just happened to be uncovered somehow, and if she just happened to be close enough to keep them warm, that probably wouldn't be the worst thing in the world either (Ruth 3:1–5). But she wasn't to go too far. Back in Jericho, Boaz's mother, Rahab (q.v.), had had a rather seamy reputation for going too far professionally, and anything that re-minded him of that might scare him off permanently.

Ruth followed her mother-in-law's advice to the letter, and it worked like a charm. Boaz was so overwhelmed that she'd pay attention to an old crock like him when there were so many young bucks running around in tight-fitting jeans that he fell for her hook, line, and sinker, and after a few legal matters were taken care of, made her his lawful wedded wife.

They had a son named Obed after a while, and Naomi came to take care of him and stayed on for the rest of her life. Then in time Obed had a son of his own named Jesse, and Jesse in turn had seven sons, the seventh of whom was named David and ended up as the greatest king Israel ever had. With Ruth for his great-grandmother and Naomi for his grandfather's nurse, it was hardly a wonder.

(The Book of Ruth)

Ss

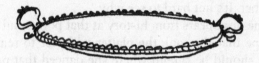

SALOME

One of the less offensive acts of King Herod Antipas (q.v.) was to walk off with his brother's wife, Herodias—at least there may have been something like love in it—but it was against the law, and since John the Baptist was a stickler for that sort of thing, he gave Herod a hard time over it. Needless to say, this didn't endear him to Herodias, who urged her husband to make short work of him. Herod said he'd be only too pleased to oblige her, but unfortunately John was a good man with a strong following, and it might lead to unpleasantness.

Then one day he threw himself a birthday party, possibly because he couldn't locate anybody who felt like throwing it for him, and one of the guests was Herodias's daughter by her former marriage. Her name was Salome, and she was both Herod's step-daughter and his niece. As it happened, she was also a whiz at dancing. Sometime during the evening she ripped off a little number which so tickled Herod that, carried away by the general hilarity of the occasion as he was, he told her he'd give her anything she wanted up to and including half of his kingdom. Since she already had everything a girl could want and was apparently not eager for all

the headaches that taking over half the kingdom would undoubtedly involve, she went out and told her mother, Herodias, to advise her what she ought to ask for.

It didn't take Herodias twenty seconds to tell her. "The
head of John," she snapped out, so that's what Salome went
back and told Herod, adding only that she would prefer to
have it served on a platter. No sooner was it brought to her
than she got rid of it like a hot potato by handing it over to
her mother. It's not hard to see why.

Salome disappears from history at that point, and you can
only hope that she took the platter with her to remind her
that she should be careful where she danced that particular
dance in the future, and that she should never ask her
mother's advice again about anything, and that even when
you cut a saint's head off, that doesn't mean you've heard the
last of him by a long shot.

(Mark 6:17–22)

SAMSON (*See* DELILAH)

SAMUEL (*See also* AGAG, SAUL, WITCH OF ENDOR)

Samuel was a combination prophet, judge, and one-man
band. When the old curmudgeon wasn't out in the field trying to fight off the Philistine guerrillas, he was riding his cir-
cuit trying to keep the tribes of Israel honest, and when he
wasn't doing that, he was giving them Hell for cheating on
Yahweh every time a new fertility god showed up with a
come-hither look in his eye. When he reached retirement
age, he might have turned things over to his sons, but they
were a bunch of crooks who sold justice to the highest bidder, and the Israelites said maybe he'd better get them a king
instead. They'd never had one before, but they felt the time
had come. Samuel threw a fit.

He said there was only one king worth the time of day, and
Yahweh was his name. He also told them kings were a bad lot
from the word go and didn't spare them a single sordid

detail. They were always either drafting you into their armies or strong-arming you into taking care of their farms. They took your daughters and put them to work in their kitchens and perfume factories. They filled their barns with your livestock and got you to slave for them till you dropped in your tracks. What was more, if Israel chose a king, Yahweh would wash his hands of them and good riddance. Samuel had it on the highest authority. But the Israelites insisted, and since Samuel didn't have the pep he'd once had, he finally gave in.

The king he dug up for them was a tall drink of water named Saul. He was too handsome for his own good, had a rich father, and when it came to religion, tended to go off the deep end. Samuel had him in for a meal and, after explaining the job to him, anointed him with holy oil against his better judgment and made him the first king Israel ever had. He regretted this action till the day he died, and even in his grave the memory of it never gave him a moment's peace.

(1 Samuel 8–11)

SAPPHIRA (See ANANIAS)

SARAH (See also HAGAR)

Quantitatively speaking, you don't find all that much laughter in the Bible, but, qualitatively, there's nothing quite like it to be found anywhere else. There are a couple of

chapters in the Book of Genesis that positively shake with it.
Sarah was never going to see ninety again, and Abraham had
already hit one hundred, and when the angel told them that
the stork was on his way at last, they both of them almost
collapsed. Abraham laughed "till he fell on his face" (Genesis 17:17), and Sarah stood cackling behind the tent door so
the angel wouldn't think she was being rude as the tears
streamed down her cheeks. When the baby finally came,
they even called him Laughter—which is what Isaac means
in Hebrew—because obviously no other name would do.

Laughter gets mixed up with all sorts of things in the Bible
and in the world too, things like sneering, irony, making fun
of, and beating the competition hollow. It also gets mixed up
with things like comedians and slipping on banana peels and
having the soles of your feet tickled. There are times when
you laugh to keep from crying like when the old wino stag-
gers home in a party hat, or even in the midst of crying like
when Charlie Chaplin boils his shoe for supper because he's
starving to death. But one hundred percent, bonded, aged-
in-the-wood laughter is something else again.

It's the crazy parrot-squawks that issue out of David as he
spins like a top in front of the Ark (2 Samuel 6:16–21). It's
what the psalms are talking about where they say, "When the
Lord had rescued Zion, then our mouth was filled with

laughter" (Psalm 126:1–2), or where they get so excited they yell out, "Let the floods clap their hands, let the hills sing for joy together!" because the Lord has come through at last (Psalm 98:8). It's what the Lord himself is talking about when he says that on the day he laid the cornerstone of the earth "the morning stars sang together, and all the sons of God shouted for joy" (Job 38:7), and it's what the rafters ring with when the Prodigal comes home and his old crock of a father is so glad to see him he almost has a stroke and "they began to make merry" and kept on making merry till the cows came home (Luke 15:24). It's what Jesus means when he stands in that crowd of cripples and loners and oddballs and factory rejects and says, "Blessed are you that weep now, for you shall laugh" (Luke 6:21). Nobody claims there's a chuckle on every page, but laughter's what the whole Bible is really about. Nobody who knows his hat from home-plate claims that getting mixed up with God is all sweetness and light, but ultimately it's what that's all about too.

Sarah and her husband had had plenty of hard knocks in their time, and there were plenty more of them still to come, but at that moment when the angel told them they'd better start dipping into their old age pensions for cash to build a nursery, the reason they laughed was that it suddenly dawned on them that the wildest dreams they'd ever had hadn't been half wild enough.

(Genesis 17, 18, 21)

SAUL (See also AGAG, JONATHAN, SAMUEL, WITCH OF ENDOR)

Saul, the first king of Israel, had three things going against him almost from the beginning. One of them was the prophet Samuel, another was a young man named David, and the third and worst was himself.

Samuel never thought Israel should have had a king in the first place and told him so at regular intervals. After Saul defeated the Amalekites, Samuel said the rules of the game

were that he should take the whole pack of them plus their king and all their livestock and sacrifice them to Yahweh. When Saul decided to sacrifice only the sway-backs and runts of the litter, keeping the cream of the crop and the king for himself (*see* AGAG), Samuel said it was the last straw and that Yahweh was through with him for keeps. Samuel then snuck off and told a boy named David that he was to be the next king, and the sooner the better. In the meanwhile, however, they both kept the matter under their hats.

Saul was hit so hard by the news that Yahweh was through with him that his whole faith turned sour. The God he'd always loved became the God who seemed to have it in for him no matter what he did or failed to do, and he went into such a state of depression that he could hardly function. The only person who could bring him out of it was this same David. He was a good-looking young red-head with a nice voice and would come and play songs on his lyre till the king's case of the horrors was under at least temporary control. Saul lost his heart to him eventually, and when the boy knocked out the top Philistine heavy-weight (*see* GOLIATH), their relationship seemed permanently cinched.

It wasn't. David could charm the birds out of the trees, and soon all Israel was half in love with him. "Saul has slain his thousands and David his ten thousands," the ladies would dither every time he rounded the bend in his fancy uniform (1 Samuel 18:7), and Saul began to smoulder. It was one day when David was trying to chase his blues away with some new songs that he burst into flame. He heaved his spear at him and just missed by a quarter of an inch. When his own son and heir, Jonathan (q.v.), fell under David's spell too, that did it. It was love-hate from then on.

He hated him because he needed him, and he needed him because he loved him, and when he wasn't out to kill him every chance he got, he was hating himself for his own evil disposition. One day he went into a cave to take a leak, not knowing that David was hiding out there, and while he was taking forty winks afterwards, David snipped off a piece of his cloak. When David produced the snippet later to prove he could have tried to kill him in return but hadn't, Saul said, "Is this your voice, my son David?" and wept as if his heart would break (1 Samuel 24). It was exactly what, in the end, his heart did.

He was told in advance that he was going to lose the battle of Gilboa and die in the process (see WITCH OF ENDOR), but in spite of knowing that, or maybe because of it, he went ahead and fought it anyway.

There are two versions of what happened to him then. One is that after being badly wounded by arrows, he persuaded a young Amalekite to put him out of his misery. The other is that he took his own sword and fell on it. In either case, it is hard to hold it against him for tendering back to the God he had once loved a life that for years he had found unbearable.

(1 Samuel 9–30)

SHADRACH, MESHACH, AND ABEDNEGO
(See NEBUCHADNEZZAR)

SIMEON

Jesus was still in diapers when his parents brought him to the Temple in Jerusalem "to present him to the Lord" (Luke 2:22), as the custom was, and offer a sacrifice, and that's

when old Simeon spotted him. Years before, he'd been told he wouldn't die till he'd seen the Messiah with his own two eyes, and time was running out. When the moment finally came, one look through his cataract lenses was all it took. He asked if it would be all right to hold the baby in his arms, and they told him to go ahead but be careful not to drop it.

"Lord, now lettest thou thy servant depart in peace, according to thy word, for mine eyes have seen thy salvation," he said (Luke 2:29), the baby playing with the fringes of his beard. The parents were pleased as punch, and so he blessed them too for good measure. Then something about the mother stopped him, and his expression changed.

What he saw in her face was a long way off, but it was there so plainly he couldn't pretend. "A sword will pierce through your soul," he said (Luke 2:35).

He would rather have bitten off his tongue than said it, but in that holy place he felt he had no choice. Then he handed her back the baby and departed in something less than the perfect peace he'd dreamed of all the long years of his waiting.

(Luke 2:22–35)

SIMON MAGUS

Simon Magus lived in Samaria and was the Houdini of his day. He made small boys climb ropes and disappear. He sawed pretty girls in half. He pulled rabbits out of hats and levitated volunteers from the audience. And he made a good thing of it too. He got top billing, drove a Cadillac to work, and wore nothing but silk next to his skin.

Then one day Philip came to town on a preaching junket, and Simon Magus got religion in a big way. When the altar call was given, he was the first to come forward. He then got himself baptized, and Philip added him to the team.

After a while the apostle Peter came down from the head office in Jerusalem to see how things were going, and before he was through, he conferred the power of healing on some of them by laying his hands on their heads. The healings struck Simon Magus as the most spectacular tricks he had ever seen in his life, and he offered Peter hard cash if he'd lay his hands on him.

God didn't belong to the magicians' union, Peter told him, and as for the hard cash, he knew what he could do with it. He said that maybe if Simon Magus repented, God would overlook what had happened, but he didn't make the prospects sound too hopeful. There might still be Hell to pay.

Knowing when he'd been upstaged, Simon Magus begged Peter to use his influence with the Lord to get him off the hook and then steered clear of the old fisherman for the remainder of his visit.

(Acts 8:5–24)

SOLOMON (*See also* HIRAM, QUEEN OF SHEBA)

King Solomon was a product of the scandalous liaison between King David and Uriah's wife Bathsheba (q.v.). It was not an auspicious beginning. He was then brought up in that hot-bed of oriental intrigue and ostentation that was his father's court, and that was less than conducive to the development of sound moral character. He also spent his formative years under the thumb of his beautiful but conniving mother who had browbeaten David on his death-bed into giving him the throne in the first place. It is a wonder he turned out as well as he did.

He was the first of the big-time spenders, and the menu that he and his retinue consumed *per diem* reads like the inventory of General Foods: a thousand measures of flour and meal plus ten oxen, twenty steers, and one hundred sheep, not to mention a garnishing of harts, gazelles, roebucks, and butter-ball chickens for when their jaded palates were in need of reupholstering. He had forty thousand horses with twelve thousand horsemen to keep them in shape, and recent excavations of his stables indicate that these figures aren't as far out of line as they might seem. His building program isn't to be overlooked either.

He put up a Temple in Jerusalem that had to be seen to be believed. It stood three stories high, and you entered it through a soaring porch of Egyptian design that was flanked by two thirty-foot free-standing bronze columns with carved lilies on top. It had cedar ceilings, cypress floors, and olivewood doors, and the amount of gold they used to trim it inside and out would have bankrupted Fort Knox. Seven years was what it took him to finish this job for God, and he then proceeded to build a palace for himself which took thirteen. It was composed of the House of the Forest of Lebanon, the Hall of Pillars, the Hall of the Throne, and the Hall of Judgment. These were for show. He also had them knock together a nice little place for his personal use and another for his wife, the daughter of Pharaoh.

The daughter of Pharaoh was not his only wife. Perhaps the reason they preferred separate bedrooms was that he had six hundred and ninety-nine more. Just in case they all happened to be busy at the same time some evening, he also had three hundred other ladies who were ready to drop everything for him at a moment's notice. Some of these were Moabites or Ammonites, some were Edomites or Sidonians, and there were five or six dozen Hittites thrown in to round things out. It was a regular smorgasbord.

Somehow he found time to run the country too, and in some ways he didn't make too bad a job of it. His reign lasted forty years, and Israel was at peace the whole time. He made advantageous treaties with both Egypt and Tyre, and in partnership with Hiram, King of Tyre, maintained a fleet of ocean-going ships that did a brisk export-import business with a number of Mediterranean ports, dealing in things like gold, silver, ivory, apes, and peacocks. He also made a killing as a horse-trader.

Unfortunately the price for all this ran pretty high, and it was his subjects who had to pick up the tab. In order to finance his building program he had to bleed them white with tolls and taxes. In order to get people to man the bulldozers and bench saws, he had to press them into forced labor gangs. You don't keep seven hundred wives and three hundred lady friends happy on peanuts either, and it was the people who had to foot that bill too. When some of them revolted in the north under the leadership of Jeroboam, he managed to quash it successfully, but instead of solving the problem, that just postponed it.

Furthermore, his taste for foreign ladies got him into more kinds of trouble than just financial. They worshiped a whole carnival of fancy foreign gods, and in his old age Solomon decided to play it safe by seeing to it that not one of them went neglected. He put up expensive altars to Ashtoreth of the Sidonians, Milcom of the Ammonites, and Chemoth of the Moabites, to name just a few, and Yahweh was so furious he said it was only for his father David's sake that he didn't settle Israel's hash right then and there. As it was, he said he'd wait a few years.

In spite of everything, Solomon was famous for his great wisdom. There wasn't a riddle he couldn't crack with one hand tied behind him (see HIRAM, QUEEN OF SHEBA), and he tossed off so many *bon mots* in the course of a day that it reached the point where people figured that if anything clever was said anywhere, it must have been Solomon who originally said it, and the whole Book of Proverbs was ascribed to his hand. His judgments in court were also praised to the skies, the most famous of them involving a couple of chippies each of whom claimed to be the mother of the same child, to which Solomon proposed the simple solution of slicing the child down the middle and giving each one half. When the first girl said that was fine by her and the second girl said she'd rather lose the case, Solomon awarded the child to the second girl, and it was all over Jerusalem within the hour.

But wisdom is more than riddles and wisecracks and court-room technique, and in most things that mattered King Solomon was among the wisest fools who ever wore a crown. He didn't even have the wit to say, *"Après moi, le déluge"* in Hebrew and was hardly cold in his grave when revolution split the country in two. From there on out the history of Israel was an almost unbroken series of disasters.

(1 Kings 3–11)

STEPHEN

After Jesus died, it took a while for his followers to settle down and get organized, and the process was no easier then than it has been ever since. One problem that came up early in the game was how to take care of the poor, especially the widows who couldn't support themselves. The apostles decided to appoint a group to handle this side of things, and one of the ones they appointed was Stephen.

His career was a short one. In addition to doing what he could for the poor, he also did what he could to spread the word about Jesus, the one who'd gotten him interested in the poor in the first place. He healed, and he preached, and he talked about how his own life had been changed, and it wasn't long before the Jewish authorities called him on the mat to defend his far-out views as best he could. As far as they were concerned, he was a bad apple.

Stephen made them a long speech, the gist of which was that from the year One the Jews had always been an ornery lot, "stiff-necked," he said, and circumcised as all get-out in one department but as cussed and mean as everybody else in all the others (Acts 7:51). They'd given Moses a hard time in the wilderness, he said, and there hadn't been a saint or prophet since that they hadn't had it in for. The way they'd treated Jesus was the last and worst example of how they were always not just missing the boat but doing their damndest to sink it. The authorities were naturally enraged and illustrated the accuracy of Stephen's analysis by taking him out and stoning him to death.

Stoning somebody to death, especially somebody as young and healthy as Stephen, isn't easy. You don't get the job done with the first few rocks and broken bottles, and even after you've got the man down, it's a long, hot business. To prepare themselves for the work-out, they stripped to the waist and got somebody to keep an eye on their things till they were through. The man they got was a fire-breathing young arch-conservative Jew named Saul, who was there because he thoroughly approved of what they were doing.

It was a scene that Saul never forgot. Years later when he'd become a Christian himself and was under arrest much as Stephen had been, he spoke of it. He wasn't called Saul any more by then but Paul (q.v.), the apostle to the Gentiles, the great letter-writing saint, and he still remembered how it had been that day when he'd stood guard over the pile of coats and ties and watched a young man's death.

Stephen was the first person to shed blood for the new faith he loved more than his life, and as Saul-who-was-to-become-Paul watched the grim process, it never occurred to him that by the grace of God the time was not far off when he himself would be another.

(Acts 6–7, 22:20)

SUSANNA

Susanna and Bathsheba had a number of points in common. Both of them were very beautiful, both were married, and both had the fatal habit of taking their baths out of doors. Both of them also had the misfortune to arouse, through no fault of their own, the baser passions of the male animal. But there the resemblance ends. How Bathsheba responded to the advances of King David is recorded under her name. Susanna was a different kind of woman.

In her case, it was not a young king who lusted after her charms but a couple of old goats. They were not only friends of her husband's but judges to boot, and in both capacities they ought to have known better. Each of them, unknown to the other, used to keep himself in a state of perpetual excitement by spying on her as she took her noonday strolls in her

husband's garden, and one day when they happened to col-
lide among the shrubbery, they confessed to each other their
common passion and cooked up a sordid little plan.

It was a hot afternoon, and Susanna, having first modestly
dismissed her two maids and told them to be sure to latch
the gate on their way out, undressed and started bathing in
the garden pool. She had no idea that the two were crouch-
ing in the bushes, and as soon as she was alone, they
emerged and confronted her.

It is a haunting scene—the slim girl floating like a lily
under the blue sky and the two old lechers standing there at
the water's edge in the rusty black gowns of their profession.
Either she was to let them have their way with her then and
there, they said, or they would swear under oath they'd
caught her in the act with a young lover and get her stoned
to death. Though the temptation must have been consider-
able to save her skin instead of her honor, she turned them
down cold. The next day, despite her protestations of inno-
cence, the testimony of her two accusers was believed, and
she was led off to her execution. On the way, however, she
said a prayer to Yahweh, and Yahweh answered it by sending
to the rescue a young man named Daniel (q.v.).

Daniel was no lawyer, but he had some ideas of his own
about the law. First he turned to the men who were standing
there at the ready with stones in their hands and called them
a pack of fools. Then he got permission to interrogate the
two old goats separately and asked them both the same question: Under what kind of tree had they seen Susanna and her
alleged boy friend carrying on? When one of them said it
was a mastic and the other a holm, the crowd wised up to
them at last and tossed them off the edge of a cliff. It was a
disagreeable fate, but for one thing, they'd asked for it, and
for another, maybe the shock of being thrown off a cliff isn't
all that much worse than the torments of unsatisfied desire.
At least it's over quicker.

In one sense Daniel is the hero of the tale, and in another, Yahweh is for getting him there just in time. But the real hero, of course, is Susanna herself. Though she was naked as the day she was born that time at the pool and the two dirty old men decked out like Supreme Court justices on Inauguration Day, she wore her integrity like gold lamé, and her sheer guts stripped their seaminess bare. In the event that Daniel hadn't shown up when he did, you feel that even lying dead of multiple fractures under a pile of stones she would have come out the winner, and even with their reputations still intact, the two old goats would have lost, and known they'd lost, vastly more than just the tryst they'd dreamed of with a lovely girl on a summer afternoon.

(Daniel 13—Latin Vulgate)

Tt

THOMAS

Imagination was not Thomas's long suit. He called a spade a spade. He was a realist. He didn't believe in fairy tales, and if anything else came up that he didn't believe in or couldn't understand, his questions could be pretty direct.

There was the last time he and the others had supper with Jesus, for instance. Jesus was talking about dying, and he said he would be leaving them soon, but it wouldn't be forever. He said he'd get things ready for them as soon as he got where he was going, and when their time finally came too, they'd all be together again. They knew the way he was going, he said, and some day they'd be there with him themselves.

Nobody else breathed a word, but Thomas couldn't hold back. When you got right down to it, he said, he personally had no idea where Jesus was going, and he didn't know the way to get there either. "I am the way," was what Jesus said to him (John 14:6), and although Thomas let it go at that, you can't help feeling that he found the answer less than satisfactory. Jesus wasn't a way, he was a man, and it was too bad he so often insisted on talking in riddles.

Then in the next few days all the things that everybody could see were going to happen happened, and Jesus was dead just as he'd said he'd be. That much Thomas was sure of. He'd been on hand himself. There was no doubt about it. And then the thing that nobody had ever been quite able to believe would happen happened too.

Thomas wasn't around at the time, but all the rest of them were. They were sitting crowded together in a room with the door locked and the shades drawn, scared sick they'd be the ones to get it next, when suddenly Jesus came in. He wasn't a ghost you could see the wallpaper through, and he wasn't just a figment of their imagination because they were all too busy imagining the horrors that were all too likely in store for themselves to imagine anything much about anybody else. He said *shalom* and then showed them enough of where the Romans had let him have it to convince them he was as real as they were if not more so. He breathed the Holy Spirit on them and gave them a few instructions to go with it, and then left.

Nobody says where Thomas was at the time. One good thing about not having too much of an imagination is that you're not apt to work yourself up into quite as much of a panic as Thomas's friends had, for example, and maybe he'd gone out for a cup of coffee or just to sit in the park for a while and watch the pigeons. Anyway, when he finally returned and they told him what had happened, his reaction was just about what they might have expected. He said that unless Jesus came back again so he could not only see the nail marks for himself but actually touch them, he was afraid that, much as he hated to say so, he simply couldn't believe that what they had seen was anything more than the product of wishful thinking or an optical illusion of an unusually vivid kind.

Eight days later, when Jesus did come back, Thomas was there and got his wish. Jesus let him see him and hear him and touch him, and not even Thomas could hold out against evidence like that. He had no questions left to ask and not enough energy left to ask them with even if he'd had a couple. All he could say was, "My Lord and my God!" (John 20:28), and Jesus seemed to consider that under the circumstances that was enough.

Then Jesus asked a question of his own. "Have you believed because you have seen me?" he said and then added, addressing himself to all the generations that have come since, "Blessed are those who have not seen and yet believe" (John 20:29).

Even though he said the greater blessing is for those who can believe without seeing, it's hard to imagine that there's a believer anywhere who wouldn't have traded places with Thomas, given the chance, and seen that face and heard that voice and touched those ruined hands.

(John 14:1–7, 20:19–29)

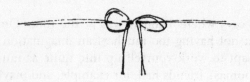

TOBIAS

Tobias was a young man when he ran into the angel Raphael, and not knowing that he was an angel at all, let alone one of seven great ones who stand and enter before the glory of the Lord, Tobias hired him at a drachma a day to be his traveling companion. Accompanied by Tobias's dog, they had a series of adventures that were nothing less than extraordinary.

Tobias almost lost his foot to a great fish. He discovered a cure for his father's blindness. He picked up a large sum of money that his father had left with a friend. And after first curing a young woman named Sarah of a demon who had caused her first seven husbands to perish on their wedding nights, he not only married her himself but lived to tell the tale.

But the best part of the story is the short, no-nonsense prayer with which he married her. "And now I take not this my sister for lust, but in truth," he said. "Command that I and she may find mercy and grow old together. Amen" (Tobit 8:8–9).

Never has the knot been more securely or simply or eloquently tied, and it's small wonder that it lasted them through a long and happy marriage that did not come to an end until Tobias died in peace at the age of one hundred and seventeen.

(The Book of Tobit)

Uu

URIAH THE HITTITE (*See also* BATHSHEBA, NATHAN)

Uriah the Hittite, Bathsheba's husband, was a straight
arrow and a patriot, and in his eyes the king could do no
wrong. There's no reason to think he had any idea David was
carrying on with Bathsheba while he was off in the army, but
you suspect that even if somebody had tipped him off about
it, he wouldn't have made all that much of a fuss.

When Bathsheba told David she was pregnant by him, he
decided to move fast and had her husband sent back from
the front on the double. His hope was that Uriah would lose
no time bedding down his beautiful bride, and that way,
when the time came, he'd have no reason for thinking the
baby was anyone's but his. But he didn't count on Uriah's

strong moral character and high sense of duty. Uriah said that as long as his troops were back there slogging it out in the trenches, he refused to live it up at home or have sex with anybody. Even after David got him all liquored up one night in an effort to lower his resistance, he still insisted on sleeping curled up on the palace floor, and Bathsheba bedded down alone.

His first trick having failed, David had Uriah bundled off to the front again with a note to General Joab saying to assign him where the fighting was fiercest. Uriah was soon shot down by the enemy, and after a long enough mourning period to make it look respectable, David married Bathsheba himself.

If Uriah could have known about the long and illustrious line that was to issue from that unseemly match, the chances are he would have considered his death none too high a price to pay. With Solomon in mind and all the mighty kings who followed him, he would probably have rejoiced in the thought that by bowing out at the right moment he had been able to give so many lives besides his own to the service of his country.

(2 Samuel 11)

VASHTI

King Ahasuerus of Persia, better known as Xerxes (q.v.), decided to throw a party that would make the Darktown Strutters' Ball look like a nursery tea. He invited not only everybody who was anybody but everybody who was nobody in particular too, and as far as expense went, the sky was the limit. It was to last for seven days, and the palace was turned upside down getting ready for it. New blue and white curtains were hung in all the windows, silver couches were moved in by the cartload, and drinks were served in goblets of pure gold. Vashti, the king's wife and queen, decided that the boys shouldn't be the only ones to enjoy themselves, so she threw a party of her own and asked in all the girls.

By the time the seventh day rolled around, the king was feeling no pain. Having shown off all his other treasures, he decided the moment had come to show off Queen Vashti, too. She was a raving beauty, and he wanted to see the rest of the boys turn green with envy when he paraded her around in front of them for a while. So he sent word to her through a couple of eunuchs to get down there in a hurry. On the grounds that she was a human being rather than a silver couch and that a woman was as good as a man any day, she refused to be trotted out as a sex-object and turned the king down flat.

Needless to say, the king was fit to be tied. Not only had he and his friends been personally insulted, but if Vashti was allowed to get away with a thing like that, who could tell what the girls would be asking for next. Maybe even the vote. Therefore he divorced her on the spot and married a lady named Esther instead.

That is how Queen Vashti lost her throne but kept her self-respect, and there seems to be absolutely no question as to which of the two she valued more highly.

(Esther 1–2)

Ww

WHALE (*See also* JONAH)

If it was actually a whale that swallowed Jonah on his voyage to Tarshish, it couldn't have been the kind of right whale you find in those waters because their gullets aren't big enough. Maybe it was a sperm whale because they can handle something the size of a prophet without batting an eye. Or maybe, since the Hebrew word means only "great fish," it wasn't a whale at all but a man-eating shark, some of whom attain lengths as great as thirty feet. But whatever it was, this much is certain.

No matter how deep it dove and no matter how dark the inside of its belly, no depth or darkness was enough to drown out the sound of Jonah's prayer. "I am cast out from thy presence. How shall I again look upon thy holy temple?" (Jonah 2:4) the intractable and water-logged old man called out from sixty fathoms, and Yahweh heard him, and answered him, and Jonah's relief at being delivered from the whale can hardly have been any greater than the whale's at being delivered from Jonah.

(Jonah 1:17–2:10)

194

WISE MEN (*See also* HEROD THE GREAT)

The gifts that the three Wise Men, or Kings, or Magi, brought to the manger in Bethlehem cost them plenty but seem hardly appropriate to the occasion. Maybe they were all they could think of for the child who had everything. In any case, they set them down on the straw—the gold, the frankincense, the myrrh—worshiped briefly, and then returned to the East where they had come from. It gives you pause to consider how, for all their great wisdom, they overlooked the one gift that the child would have been genuinely pleased to have someday, and that was the gift of themselves and their love.

(Matthew 2:1–12)

WITCH OF ENDOR

As soon as King Saul passed a law against witchcraft and drove all practitioners out of the land, the Witch of Endor traded in her broomstick on a bicycle, changed her pointed black hat for a summer straw, flushed a great many evil-smelling concoctions down the john, and tried to go straight.

But then Saul fell on evil times. He felt so sure David was after his throne that he grew paranoid on the subject. He was convinced his own son Jonathan had sided against him too. And the Philistines were gathering for a massive attack at Gilboa. He had to know how things were going to turn out, and since he and Yahweh were no longer on speaking terms

as far as he was concerned, and the prophet Samuel was dead, he was forced to go elsewhere for his information.

He tried a dream-book, but none of his dreams were in it. He tried things like tea leaves and Ouija boards, but they all malfunctioned. So he asked his servants whether they happened to know if anybody was still around who might be able to help, if they knew what he meant, and they told him about this old party in Endor who looked like something straight out of Charles Addams.

Saul disguised himself heavily for the visit, but as soon as he stepped through the door and said he wanted her to conjure up somebody who could foretell the future, she grew shrill and suspicious. What did he want to do, she said, get the fuzz after her? And only when he swore by Yahweh that he wouldn't breathe a word to a soul did she go so far as to ask him who exactly it was he'd like her to try to get hold of for him. As soon as he said Samuel, she knew there could be only one person in Israel who would dare face that fierce old ghost, and the cat was out of the bag.

"You are Saul," she said, and by that time he was past denying it. The next thing she knew, he'd let out a yelp that not only was enough to awaken the dead but did. "An old man is coming up, and he is wrapped in a robe," she said, and Saul realized immediately he was the right old man and bowed so low his beard touched the carpet (1 Samuel 28:12–14).

Except on the grounds of wanting to make himself even more miserable than he already was, it's hard to explain why it was his old enemy he'd asked for. Even before Samuel opened his mouth, Saul knew what he was going to say, and sure enough he said it. Samuel told him that everybody was against him including Yahweh, and not only would the Philistines win at Gilboa but by that time the next day Saul and all his sons would be joining him in the grave. Saul crumpled in a heap to the floor.

The witch did all she could to get him back on his feet. She tried to make him eat something, but he refused. She told him that she'd done what he'd asked her and the least he could do in return was take enough to get his strength back and go, but he didn't even seem to hear what she was saying. Finally with the help of the servants she managed to get him to where he was sitting on the edge of the bed (1 Samuel 28:23), and when she produced a little meat and some freshly baked bread, he stuffed a bit of it into his mouth and then left without saying a word.

Nobody knows what the witch did after they were gone. Probably she just sat there in a daze for a while, trying to pull herself together with the comforting smell of the bread she'd baked. Maybe she decided to get out of Endor for good in case Saul broke his word and squealed on her. But she needn't have worried about that because Saul had no time left to squeal on anybody.

On the next day he was just as dead as Samuel had risen from the grave to tell him he'd be, and this side of Paradise or anywhere else, she'd never have to worry about seeing him again. Unless she got herself talked into having another seance, of course, but the odds against that seem overwhelming.

(1 Samuel 28)

Xx

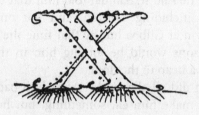

XERXES (*See also* VASHTI)

King Xerxes of Persia, otherwise known as Ahasuerus, has the distinction of being the only person in the Bible whose name begins with an X. There's not much else you can say for him. He was a blow-hard and a show-off, and anybody with an eighth-grade education could wrap him around his little finger without half trying. Or *her* little finger.

There was Haman, for example. Haman was Xerxes' right-hand man and a raging anti-Semite. There was also a Jew named Mordecai, who lived in the capital, and one day when Haman came prancing by, Mordecai refused to flatten himself out and grovel in the dust like everybody else. It was the break Haman had been waiting for. He told Xerxes about Mordecai's insubordination and rudeness and said it was a vivid illustration of how the Jews as a whole were a miserable lot. He said if you let one of them in, they brought their friends, and Persia was crawling with them. He said the only laws they respected were their own, and it was obvious they didn't give a hoot in Hell about the king or anybody else. He then said that as far as he was concerned, the only thing to do was exterminate the whole pack of them like rats and of-

fered the king ten thousand of the best for the privilege of or-
ganizing the operation. Xerxes pocketed the cash and told
him to go ahead.

But then there was also Queen Esther, a good-looking
Jewish girl who was both a cousin of Mordecai's and Xerxes'
second wife. As soon as she got wind of what Haman was up
to, she decided to do what she could to save her people from
the gas-chamber. Xerxes had a rather short fuse, and you had
to know how to handle him, but she planned her strategy
carefully, and by the time she was through, she'd not only
talked him out of letting the Jews get exterminated but had
gotten him to hang Haman from the same gallows that had
been set up for Mordecai. She even managed to persuade
Xerxes to give Mordecai Haman's old job.

Unfortunately, the end of the story is less edifying. Not
content with having saved their people and taken care of
Haman, Esther and Mordecai used their new power to or-
chestrate the slaughter of seventy-five thousand of their old
enemies. The whole unpleasant account is contained in the
Book of Esther, which has the distinction of being the only
book in the Bible where the name of God isn't even mentioned. There seems every reason to believe that he considered himself well out of it.

(The Book of Esther)

Yy

YAHWEH

Yahweh is one of God's names, and Moses was the first one he told it to. Maybe it means "I am what I am" or something along those lines, and maybe it doesn't. At other places in the Bible he is given names like Elohim, El Shaddai, the Lord. Jesus called him mainly Abba, which is Aramaic for *father*. Yahweh doesn't seem to care too much what people call him as long as the lines of communication are kept open.

He "inhabits eternity," says the prophet Isaiah (Isaiah 57:15). That means before there was anything, he was, and long after there's nothing much left, he still will be. But you can't apply tenses like *was* or *will be* to Yahweh literally any more than you can apply the names of colors literally to the sounds of the Royal Scots Dragoon Guards playing *Amazing Grace*. He doesn't inhabit time like everybody else. He invented time.

"If I take the wings of the morning and dwell in the uttermost parts of the sea, even there thy hand shall lead me," says the 139th Psalm (9–10), which means that any place you can possibly think of is a place where Yahweh is because there's no place you can possibly think of that's a place where

Yahweh isn't. He no more exists in space than Norman Rockwell exists in the covers of *The Saturday Evening Post*. Space is the canvas he paints creation on.

But all this doesn't mean for one second that he doesn't keep on turning up in time and space anyway. On the contrary, that's what the whole Bible is all about. Adam and Eve heard the sound of him "walking in the garden in the cool of the day," says Genesis (3:8), and one way or another he's been down here throwing his weight around ever since. He sounds off through prophets. He raises Cain through kings. He leaves all the splendor and power of nature for his calling card and makes the whole thing fresh, like bread, every time the sun rises. He makes himself known through the best impulses and wildest longings of the human heart, and Saint Paul goes even so far as to say that when people bog down in their prayers, "the Spirit himself intercedes for us with sighs too deep for words" (Romans 8:26).

The time he outdid himself, of course, was when "he so loved the world that he gave his only Son that whoever believes in him should not perish but have eternal life" (John 3:16). To put it another way, his final word to the world was the Word itself wearing flesh like a uniform and dwelling among us full of grace and truth (John 1:14). What is Yahweh all about and what do human beings have it in them at their best to be? Yahweh's answer to those formidable questions is not a theological blockbuster but a biological man, in a way the only real, honest-to-God man who ever was. Jesus was his name and Christ was the title that went with his job. "He who has seen me has seen the Father," Jesus said (John 14:9), and "God is love," said John (1 John 4:8); and the basic plot of the whole True Romance of history seems to be just that Love will have us lovely before he's through or split a gut trying. He will badger us, bulldoze us, clobber and cajole us till in the end we all make it "to the measure of the stature of the fullness of Christ" (Ephesians 4:13).

Even Nebuchadnezzar, you say? Even Hiram and Herod and the Queen of Sheba? Even Jacob and Jael and Judas, of all people? Is it possible that he intends to do a job on Heinrich Himmler and Genghis Khan, not to mention Groucho Marx and Madame de Pompadour and Warren Gamliel *Harding*, for Christ's sweet sake? Exactly. For Christ's sweet sake. And not the least staggering thought is that it seems he has similar plans in mind not only for the author of this outrageous compendium but for every last Jack and Jill who read it and even the ones who don't.

Nobody ever claimed it was going to be easy, least of all Jesus, who continually said to take up our crosses and follow him, not just our picnic baskets and tickets to Disneyland. A lot of barnacles are going to have to be scraped off and a lot of horse manure shoveled out and a lot of rooms stripped bare and redecorated before the final product emerges bright as a new penny, to mix a metaphor or two. But peculiar as we are, every last one of us, for reasons best known to himself Yahweh apparently treasures the whole three-ring circus, and every time we say "Thy kingdom come," it's home we're talking about, our best, last stop.

"I am the Alpha and the Omega," Yahweh says, "the beginning and the end" (Revelation 21:6), and he will have everybody aboard at last because if even just a couple of stragglers fail to show up, the party simply won't be complete without them.

Zz

ZACCHEUS

Zaccheus stood barely five feet tall with his shoes off and was the least popular man in Jericho. He was head tax-collector for Rome in the district and had made such a killing out of it that he was the richest man in town as well as the shortest. When word got around that Jesus would soon be passing through, he shinnied up into a sycamore tree so he could see something more than just the backs of other people's heads, and that's where he was when Jesus spotted him.

"Zaccheus," Jesus said, "get down out of there in a hurry. I'm spending tonight with YOU" (Luke 19:5), whereupon all Jericho snickered up their sleeves to think he didn't have better sense than to invite himself to the house of a man that nobody else would touch with a ten-foot pole.

But Jesus knew what he was doing. Zaccheus was taken so completely aback by the honor of the thing that before he had a chance to change his mind, he promised not only to turn over fifty percent of his holdings to the poor but to pay back, four to one, all the cash he'd extorted from everybody else. Jesus was absolutely delighted. "Today salvation has come to this house," he said (Luke 19:9), and since that was his specialty after all, you assume he was right.

Zaccheus makes a good one to end with because in a way he can stand for all the rest. He's a sawed-off little social disaster with a big bank account and a crooked job, but Jesus welcomes him aboard anyway, and that's why he reminds you of all the others too.

There's Aaron whooping it up with the Golden Calf the moment his brother's back is turned, and there's Jacob conning everybody including his own father. There's Jael driving a tent-peg through the head of an overnight guest, and Rahab, the first of the red-hot mamas. There's Nebuchadnezzar with his taste for roasting the opposition and Paul holding the lynch mob's coats as they go to work on Stephen. There's Saul the paranoid, and David the stud, and those mealy-mouthed friends of Job's who would probably have succeeded in boring him to death if Yahweh hadn't stepped in just in the nick of time. And then there are the ones who betrayed the people who loved them best such as Absalom and poor old Peter, such as Judas even.

Like Zaccheus, they're all of them peculiar as Hell, to put it quite literally, and yet you can't help feeling that, like Zaccheus, they're all of them somehow treasured too. Why are they treasured? Who knows? But maybe you can say at least this about it—that they're treasured less for who they are and for what the world has made them than for what they have it in them at their best to be because ultimately, of course, it's not the world that made them at all. "All the earth is mine!" says Yahweh, "and all that dwell therein," adds the Twenty-fourth Psalm, and in the long run, presumably, that goes for you and me too.

(Luke 19:1–10)